WHISPERS FROM THE FIRST CALIFORNIANS

from the First Californians

A STORY OF CALIFORNIA'S FIRST PEOPLE

BY
GAIL FABER and **MICHELE LASAGNA**

MAGPIE PUBLICATIONS/ALAMO, CALIFORNIA

DEDICATED TO ALL THE CALIFORNIA INDIANS
WHO SHARED THEIR HERITAGE WITH US
AND HELPED US HEAR
THE WHISPERS OF THE FIRST CALIFORNIANS.

They took their strength from the soil
and stood proud and majestic as a symbol
of the Great Spirit's love for the earth.

ACKNOWLEDGEMENTS

The authors give special thanks to the following persons for their particular contributions to this book:

Jeanne Aitken, Andrew Andreoli, Nell Barker, Rachel Ann Joseph Bluestone, Nancy DiMaggio, Loretta Head, Walt Hanson, William Johnson, Frank F. Latta, Ed Mata, Henry Mauldin, Monna Olson, Jane Penn, Harold Smith, Jimmy Toote, and Frank Ventgen.

First Edition August 1980
Second Edition August 1981

Third Edition August 1983
Fourth Edition August 1984

Published by Magpie Publications
Box 636
Alamo, Ca. 94507
ISBN: 0-936480-00-9 (student edition–soft cover)
ISBN: 0-936480-02-5 (student edition–hard cover)
ISBN: 0-936480-01-7 (teacher edition)

Dear Reader,

While teaching California history and the story of the California Indians, we became aware of a lack of materials appropriate for young people. We began to write a basic guide for young people and develop enrichment tasks that would give students a closer look at the lives of the first Californians.

In the process of writing *WHISPERS*, we have come to realize that learning about the California Indians is more than reading books, viewing artifacts in museums or attending an Indian fair. The Indian way of life is so in tune with nature that in order to learn their ways and customs you must allow the Indian spirit to become a part of you. When you see the blue sky, the raindrops, the fog, the sunset and the mighty oaks, you should remember that the Indians' spirit is a part of all these things.

We hope that this book will provide some factual information as well as give each person who reads it a deeper understanding and appreciation for the first people of California.

The Authors

TABLE OF CONTENTS

CHAPTER FOUR
NATURE'S NOURISHMENT
HUNTING AND FISHING

CHAPTER FIVE
USING NATURE'S GIFTS FOR
BASKETS, BOWLS AND BOATS

CHAPTER SIX
CLOTHING OF THE INDIANS

CHAPTER SEVEN
HOMES OF THE INDIANS

CHAPTER EIGHT
CUSTOMS, CEREMONIES AND GAMES

CHAPTER NINE
ISHI, A SPECIAL CALIFORNIAN

FIRST WHISPERS

Everything was quiet. The chill of the morning air was as yet unbroken by the cry of a bird or animal. Wisps of damp fog drifted through the sleeping foothills and clung to the meadow grass. The treetops along the ridge shone with a soft golden glow as the sun's rays began to bring warmth to nature's world. Bit by bit, sound by sound, nature shed its shadowy blanket of night to welcome the dawning of a California morning.

As the mist cleared, the whispers of nature were joined by the whispers of human voices. Silhouetted against the velvety green slopes of the foothills stood a small group of people—the first Californians. Their eyes followed the flight of a radiant butterfly as it floated over a field of wildflowers. The quiet was undisturbed except for the noisy chatter of magpies searching for berries and seeds in a nearby thicket. A jackrabbit scurried into the shadows, unaccustomed to the sound of human voices. Through this unfolding scene of beauty, nature whispered its welcome to the first Californians.

No one knows when these first people came to California. No one knows just what happened when they did come, but we do know that long, long ago there were no people living in California. There were no people on the whole North American continent! California belonged to the birds, animals, fish, trees, wind, snow and the rain. It belonged to the grass, wildflowers, rocks, oceans, streams, valleys, mountains, sunsets, clouds and skies!

CHAPTER ONE

A NEW WORLD

CREATION LEGENDS OF THE CALIFORNIA INDIANS

The California Indians tell many different stories of how their people were created and placed in this land. These are called **creation legends** and some are quite long. Tribes throughout California tell creation stories that have been passed down from **generation to generation** by the elders of the tribe. When these elders talked, everyone listened for these ancients knew the songs and stories of their people.

Indians have many creation stories and they can be told endlessly. The storyteller would tell detail after detail as the story progressed. There were many, many creation legends because the Indians told a story about each land, sea and sky animal. These legends were beautiful and creative.

* * * *

A CREATION LEGEND FROM NORTHERN CALIFORNIA

The Northern California Indians, such as the Karok, Yurok and Hupa, tell this legend about the formation of the earth and the creation of the people. The story tells how the earth was formed and then how Nagaicho returned to the North after his work on earth was finished.

*THE EARTH DRAGON

"Before this world was formed, it is said, there was another world. The sky of that world was made of Sandstone rock. Two gods, Thunder and Nagaicho, looked at the old sky because it was being shaken by Thunder.

'The Rock is old,' they said. 'We will fix it. We will stretch it out far to the East.'

Then they stretched the Sandstone rock of the sky, walking on the sky as they did so. Under each of the four corners of the sky they set a great rock to hold it. They then made the different things which would make the world pleasant for people to live in. In the South they made flowers, in the East they made a large opening so the clouds could come through, then, in the West they made an opening so the fog from the ocean could come through. To make clouds, they lit the fire. They said the clouds would keep people, who were to be made later, from having headaches because of too much sunshine.

Then, they made Man from Earth. They put grass inside of him to form his stomach. They put the figure to make Man's heart. For his liver they used a round piece of red clay, and the same for his kidneys. For his windpipe they used a reed. Then they prepared blood for Man by red stone, which they pounded into powder and mixed with water.

After making the various parts of Man, the two gods took one of his legs, split it and made Woman of it.

Then they made the Sun to travel by day; the Moon to travel by night.

But the creations of the two gods were not to endure because flood waters came. Every day it rained, every night it rained, all the People slept, and then the sky

---

*The Legend, "The Earth Dragon", is quoted exactly as it is printed in the Humboldt County Office of Education N.I.C.E. program.

fell. The waters of the oceans came together everywhere. There was no land or mountains or rocks, only water. Trees and grass were not. There were no fish or land animals or birds, as Human Beings and animals alike had been washed away. The wind did not then blow through the portals of the world, nor was there snow, nor frost, nor rain. It did not thunder nor did it lightning. Since there were no trees to be struck, it did not thunder. There was neither clouds, nor fog, nor was there a sun. It was very dark.

Then it was that this earth with its great long horns, got up and walked down this way from the North. As it walked along the deep places, and looked up, the water rose to its shoulders. When it came up into shallower places and looking up, raised the ridge in the North upon which the waves break. He came to the middle of the world, into the East, and to the rising of the Sun, Earth looked up again. There, where it looked up, a large land appeared near to the coast. Far away to the South, Earth continued looking up, and walked under the ground.

Having come from the North and traveled far South, and laid down; the God, Nagaicho, who, standing on Earth's head, had been carried to the South where the Earth now lays down. Placing Earth's head as it should be, Nagaicho spread gray clay between Earth's eyes and on each horn. Upon the clay he placed a layer of reeds, and another layer of clay. And on this he placed grass and brush and trees.

'I have finished,' Nagaicho stated. 'Let there be mountain peaks here on his head. Let the waves of the sea break against them.'

The mountains formed, banks formed on them. The small stones he had placed on Earth's head which was buried from sight, became larger.

At this time People appeared. People all had animal names and later when Indians came to live on this Earth, the First People were changed into animals which still bear their names. Seal, Sea Lion and Grizzly Bear built the Ant's house. One Woman was named Whale. She was fat and that is why there are so many stout Indian women today.

Nagaicho caused different sea food to grow, and also Abalones and Mussels and many other things of the sea grew. He then made Salt from the ocean foam. He made the waters of the ocean rise up in waves and said the ocean should always behave in that way. He said that old Whales would float ashore so People might have them to eat.

He made Redwoods and other trees grow on the tail of the Great Dragon which laid to the North.

He made creeks by dragging his foot through the Earth so People would have good fresh water to drink.

He traveled all over the Earth making things so this Earth would be a comfortable place for Man.

He had a great many Oak trees so People would have plenty of Acorns to eat.

When he had finished making everything, he and his Dog took a walk all over the Earth to see how all the new things looked. Finally, when they arrived at their starting point, he said to his Dog, 'We are close to home, my Dog. Now we should go back North and stay there.' So he left this world, where People live and now lives in the North."

* * * * *

A CREATION LEGEND FROM SOUTH CENTRAL CALIFORNIA

The legend that follows is from the Salinan Indians of South Central California. It tells of the beginning of the world and the creation of men and women. This legend is very long and only a part of it is included here.

*THE BEGINNING OF THE WORLD

"After the deluge the eagle wished to get some earth. First, duck dove into the water but failed to bring up any earth. Then the eagle put a heavy weight on the back of the kingfisher and he dove into the water for the earth and succeeded in reaching the bottom. The sea was so deep that when he came to the surface, he was dead. Between his claws the eagle found some earth and after reviving the kingfisher he took the dirt and made the world. Then he revived all the other animals who had been drowned in the deluge, the coyote next after the kingfisher. When the coyote found himself alive again, he shouted out for joy and ran around reviving the rest of the animals that he found dead, sending them back to the eagle."

*THE CREATION OF MEN AND WOMEN

"When the world was completed, there was as yet no people, but the eagle was the chief of the animals. He saw that the world was incomplete and decided to make some people. From some of the earth brought up by the kingfisher he modeled the figure of a man and laid him on the ground. In the beginning he was very small but grew rapidly until he reached normal size. But as yet, he had no life; he was still asleep. Then the eagle stood and admired his work. 'It is impossible,' said he, 'that he should be left alone; he must have a mate.' So he pulled out a feather and laid it beside the sleeping man. Then he left them and went off a short distance, for he knew that a woman was being formed from the feather. But the man was still asleep and did

*The legends, "The Beginning of the World" and the "Creation of Men and Women", (Collected by Dr. H. W. Henshaw, 1884), are quoted exactly as they are printed in the book entitled **The Salinan Indians of California** by Betty War Brusa, published by Naturegraph Publishers, Inc.

not know what was happening. When the eagle decided that the woman was about completed, he returned, awoke the man by flapping his wings over him and flew away.

The man opened his eyes and stared at the woman. 'What does this mean?' he asked. 'I thought I was alone!' Then the eagle returned and said with a smile, 'I see you have a mate!' Then he sent the newly-made couple out into the world."

* * * * *

A CREATION LEGEND FROM SOUTHERN CALIFORNIA

The Cahuilla Indians of Southern California tell this creation legend. It tells the story of the first people and how UM NAW, the Great Spirit of the land, the earth, the water, the air, watches his people, their lives, their living, their food, their homes.

*THE CREATION

"In the beginning there was nothing but nights, and other Indian words call them the two nights—man and woman . . . They tried to produce a child, but the child was lost before time for its birth. For four times the same happened and then with a flash of lightning came strong twin boys.

The name of the first one was Mo-Cot, and the name of the second was Mo-Cot-tem-ma-ya-wit, meaning creator. These were the first people. They were sitting in the air. There was no earth, no water, no light,

---

*The legend, "The Creation", is quoted exactly as it is printed in the book entitled **Stories and Legends of the Palm Springs Indians** by Chief Francisco Patencio, published by Palm Springs Desert Museum.

nothing but darkness; so they could not see each other, but they could hear each other. They did not call each other 'brother', but 'my man.'

Now this Mo-Cot, he asked, 'What are we going to do, my man?'

Mo-Cot-tem-ma-ya-wit answered, 'You should know, my man.'

Mo-Cot said, 'We must create now.'

Then Mo-Cot created first tobacco. And Mo-Cot-tem-ma-ya-wit invented the pipe and gave it two names; Man and Woman. . .

. . . Together they made a Who-Ya-No-Hut. This is like a bishop's staff, which is carried in the church today. This they tried to stand up, but it could not stand, because there was nothing for it to stand on. So they put a Tem Em La Wit (bedrock) to steady the Who-Ya-No-Hut, and yet it would not be steady, for it was growing up all of the time.

Now this was the first beginning of the earth. It was the foundation stone, and is in the middle of the world today. Then they created two kinds of snakes to hold it, but they could not hold it.

They made a big pile of stones and put them around the Who-Ya-No-Hut, and yet it was not steady; so they created great spiders, black ones and white ones (not the spiders of today, but the ones that live in the ends of the world), to weave threads to help hold it steady. . .

. . . So then they made Pal No Cit, the water ocean. Then they turned up the edges of the earth, so the water could not run over, and the earth became steady, as we see it today.

Mo-Cot-tem-ma-ya-wit asked Mo-Cot, 'How are we going to make No Cot Em (people) like ourselves?'

Mo-Cot answered, 'We have made the earth, two kinds: Fam Av Sil (meaning moist earth) and Pal Lis Ma Wit (meaning damp earth). Also the U Le Wit (meaning the clay earth), the Ta Vi Wit (meaning the

white clay and also the black clay, the yellow clay and
the red clay). Of this earth which we have made will
we make the people.'

. . . Then Mo-Cot and Mo-Cot-tem-ma-ya-wit saw all
the people that they had made, and they called them
No cot em and Ta ba tem, which mean, 'those that have
been created.'

. . . Now, after everything had settled and become
quiet again, the people could see well, and they saw
that they were of different color. For the white clay
had made white people, and the black clay had made
black people, and the yellow clay had made the yellow
people, and the red clay had made red people, and each
color of people went together.

Then it was that the white-clay people were not
pleased about being the only ones without color. They
cried to be dark, like the rest. They put different clay
on themselves, but it was not good. It came right off
after a while.

Then the people called to Mo-Cot that the people
were going away. The white people went first, and
Mo-Cot said, 'Let them go. They are different. They
will always be different.'

Then Mo-Cot saw in the daylight that the colored
people were fast going from him. He reached quickly
behind him and grasped the Red people. These were
the people that he kept with him. His creation children
left him and so it has been to this day, that the children go on away, instead of staying with the parents.
As things were done in the first beginning, so they
have done ever since."

   * * * * *

A SCIENTIFIC THEORY

You have just read a few creation legends of the California Indians. The Indians feel that these creation legends tell of the beginning of their lives in this world. Scientists, however, tell another story about the way the first men and women came to the North American **continent.** A scientific story is called a **theory.** A theory is something that is being explored and may not as yet be a proven fact. This scientific theory tells that the Indians walked from one continent to another on a **vast** mountainous ice bridge joining Asia and Alaska. This ice bridge, now known as the **Bering Strait,** extended from North of Wrangell Island and as far south as the Aleutian Islands—1300 miles! This is about the same distance as from Seattle, Washington to San Diego, California. People were able to cross this ice bridge because during the ice age, water did not cover this **route.** The wanderers followed icy trails across this frozen **wasteland.**

Many groups of men and women during thousands of years wandered across this ice bridge. They were searching for food and followed the **spoor** of numerous animals, large and small. During these thousands of years, these people migrated down into the Americas.

Gradually, as the ice melted, the changing water level began to cover this 1300 mile wide area. This happened approximately 6000 to 8000 years ago and the people who had crossed from Asia to Alaska were now left in North America.

Some of these people had dark or light skin, thick black hair, high cheekbones and heavy eyelids. Some were peaceful and some were warlike. They all spoke different languages. Those who spoke the same language stayed together in the same **tribe.** A tribe is a group of families living together under one leader or chief.

As these tribes moved into the Americas, their differences increased due to the **geography** of the continents. When we talk about geography, we mean the earth's mountains, rivers, valleys, climates, animal and plant life. Due to these differences in geography, each tribe lived in different ways with different **customs.** For example, differences between tribes can be seen when we study the customs and habits of the California coastal tribes **versus** the tribes of the desert.

By the time **Christopher Columbus** made his discovery of the New World in the West Indies (San Salvador), there were already about twenty million men and women living in the New World. Christopher Columbus named these **inhabitants** Indians, as he thought he had discovered islands near the country of **India.** What Columbus didn't realize was that he had discovered a **civilization** of people who had been living in the Americas for at least 50,000 years!

ARCHEOLOGICAL SITES

There are many theories and stories that tell about the first people on the North American continent. There are many **archeological sites** that scientists have **excavated.** These sites prove that Indians have been here thousands and thousands of years.

Some scientific theories state that the first people came to the North American continent across a land bridge joining Asia and Alaska.

Recently, archeologists from Riverside, near Los Angeles, discovered the oldest footprints ever found in North America. These footprints were made by a family of Indians as they walked along the banks of the Mojave River in San Bernardino County. The footprints date back more than 4,300 years!

In 1929, an archeologist from the San Diego Museum of Man, discovered a skull and some skeletal bones near the San Dieguito River in what is now the city limits of Del Mar, California. Mr. Malcolm Rogers, who made this discovery, was sure that his find was very old. A common date of 1,000 B.C. was given to his finds because at that time, there were few ways of dating ancient bones. Now, a little more than fifty years later, there are several ways to date archeological finds. These ways include **radiocarbon, geological** and **geomorphological dating methods.** The ancient bones that Mr. Rogers discovered in 1929 have now been dated at 48,000 years. This means that Indians were living in California almost *500 centuries ago*!!

These footprints of an Indian family were made about 4,300 years ago. The footprints were made after a rainstorm and were preserved in the river clay because a grass fire baked the clay and saved the prints.

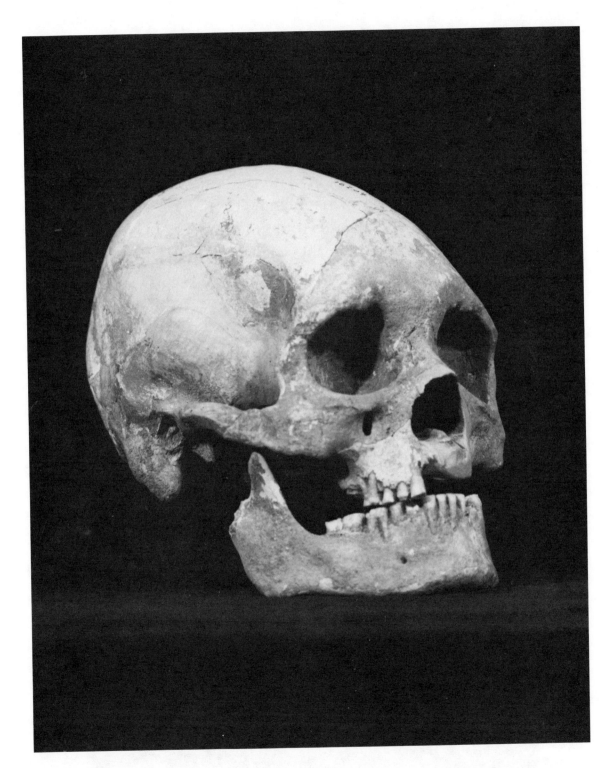

Skull found at Del Mar, California   Age: 48,000 years

INTERESTING THOUGHTS

The creation legends of the California Indians tell the beautiful stories of how the Indians came to be. The Indians believe that their beginnings lie in the earth of the California valleys, mountains and rivers created by the Great Spirit. The Indians were the first people to hear the whisperings of nature as they walked among the grasses and wildflowers of the hills and valleys. They saw the cool tule fogs drift like shimmering curtains over the mighty oaks and silent fields. They watched the droplets of dew clinging to the grasses sparkle like diamonds as golden bursts of sunlight turned the blanket of night into a new day. From the beginning, the Indians have been part of the first whispers of California. How marvelous it must be to have a heritage that reaches back in time and touches the dawning of a new world!

BACKTRACKING

Can you answer the following questions?
(1) Why do Indians tell creation legends? How do you think they were told?
(2) As the legends were told from generation to generation, do you think any of these legends might have changed? Why, or why not?
(3) Which creation legend did you like the best? Why?
(4) According to scientific theory about the Bering Strait, why did these first people migrate from their homes and come to the North American continent?
(5) What is a tribe? Are families, as we know them today, similar to tribes? How is your family similar to a tribe?
(6) How did the name "Indian" come into use?

*For Wise Eagles: What types of animals do you think were alive at the time these first people crossed the ice bridge?

*For Wise Eagles: Look up radiocarbon dating in an encyclopedia. Tell how this method determines the age of once living material.

*For Wise Eagles: Many people say that Columbus discovered the Indians.
Comment on the following statement:
The Indians discovered Columbus!

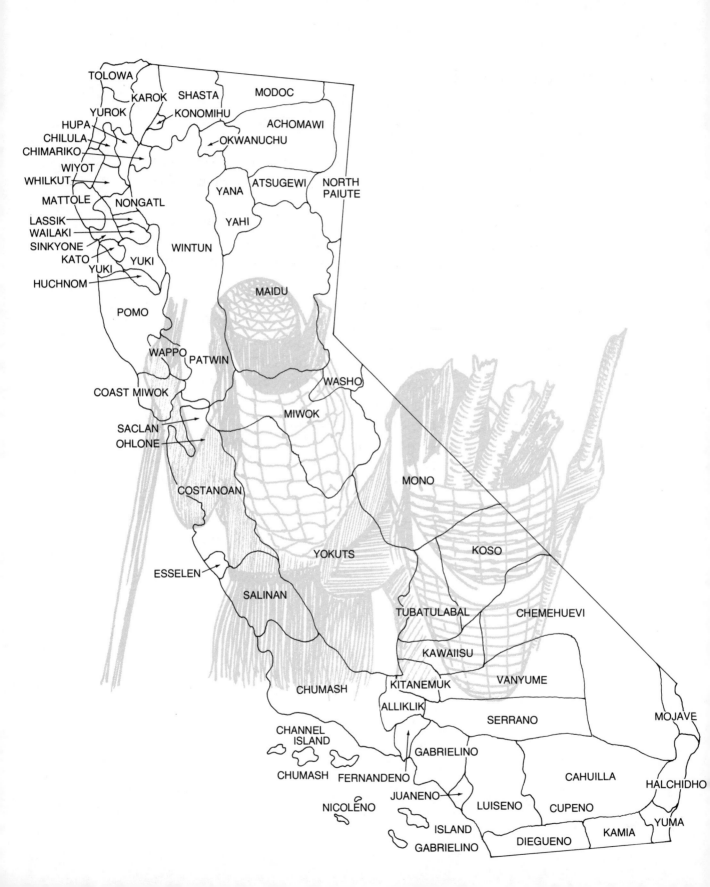

TOLOWA

KAROK SHASTA MODOC

YUROK KONOMIHU

ACHOMAWI

HUPA

CHILULA OKWANUCHU

CHIMARIKO

WIYOT

WHILKUT

YANA ATSUGEWI NORTH PAIUTE

MATTOLE NONGATL

LASSIK

WAILAKI YAHI

SINKYONE

KATO YUKI WINTUN

YUKI

HUCHNOM

MAIDU

POMO

WAPPO PATWIN

WASHO

COAST MIWOK

MIWOK

SACLAN

OHLONE

MONO

COSTANOAN

YOKUTS KOSO

ESSELEN

SALINAN

TUBATULABAL CHEMEHUEVI

KAWAIISU

VANYUME

CHUMASH KITANEMUK

ALLIKLIK

CHANNEL ISLAND SERRANO MOJAVE

GABRIELINO

CHUMASH FERNANDENO CAHUILLA HALCHIDHO

JUANENO

NICOLEÑO LUISENO CUPENO

ISLAND YUMA

GABRIELINO DIEGUENO KAMIA

CHAPTER TWO
CALIFORNIA'S FIRST INHABITANTS

WOMEN'S BELONGINGS AND TOOLS

The first people in California were the Indians. They traveled on foot. The women carried most of the belongings on their backs. Some women wore basket caps on their heads. A **tump line** or headband made of **milkweed** fiber or **nettle** fit over the cap and hung down the woman's back. This headband or tump line helped support a large **burden** basket. Other Indian women used only the tump line with no cap to support their burden baskets. Many Indian women also used a bag-like net made of milkweed, nettle or **hemp** fiber. Belongings could be carried in this net and could be used much like the backpacks of today.

The woman on the left is carrying her family's belongings in a net. Basket caps were sometimes used to prevent chafing or irritations of the skin. The woman on the right is using a headband made of plant fiber to support a burden basket on her back.

Each woman not only carried her family's belongings, but also carried her own personal belongings. Among these belongings were stirring paddles, looped sticks and a digging stick. Some women of Southern California tribes carried a small wooden paddle and a flat, smooth stone the size of a fist, for shaping and smoothing clay bowls and jars.

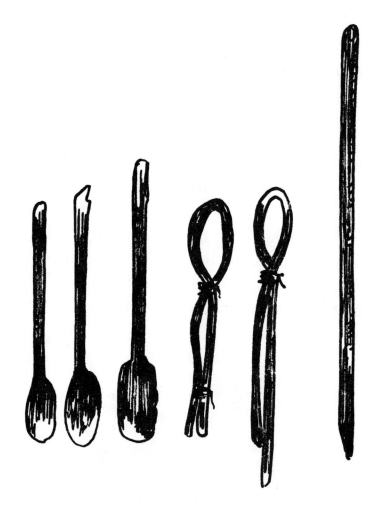

These are Indian women's belongings and working tools. The first three tools are wooden paddles used for stirring boiling mush in a cooking basket. The next two tools are looped sticks for lifting hot rocks from the fire, and for putting the rocks into the water or mush. The digging stick was used for digging roots and loosening dirt.

MEN'S BELONGINGS AND TOOLS

Among the men's belongings were bows and arrows, a skin or fur **quiver** for carrying arrows, a deer antler or stone wedge for splitting wood, a bone awl for punching holes in leather, a bone needle for sewing skins, a stick and flat piece of wood for starting a fire and a sharp pointed bone for chipping **chert** or **obsidian** or **jasper.**

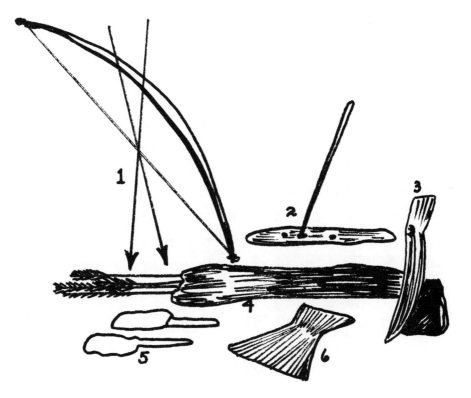

These are Indian men's belongings. Included are (1) bow and arrows (2) wood and drilling stick for starting a fire (3) elk antler wedge (4) quiver and arrows (5) awls (6) stone wedge for splitting logs.

BOWS AND ARROWS

The most important tools used by the Indians were the bow and arrow. Indian men took special care of their bows and arrows.

Bows were made from sturdy pieces of wood and were often polished with deer bone **marrow** to keep them in good condition. Sometimes one man in a tribe was especially good at making bows. He would make bows for other members of his tribe and was often such a popular craftsman that Indians from neighboring tribes traded or paid for these special bows.

Arrows were also very important. There were many different types of **arrowshafts**, but most Indians used two-piece arrows. The main shaft of the arrow was sometimes made of cane, where available, and the hunter could fit a shorter piece of wood or **foreshaft** into the hollow end of the cane. An **arrowhead** was tied to this end. The Indians who used a foreshafted arrow found it valuable because when the arrow was shot into an animal, only the main shaft need be removed and another foreshaft attached in order for the hunter to shoot again. If an arrowhead was ruined, the hunter only lost the foreshaft of the arrow and not the entire shaft.

A Hupa bow

This is the skin of a raccoon. It was used as a quiver for carrying arrows.

There were many different types of arrowshafts, but most Indians used two-piece arrows. The main shaft of the arrow was sometimes made out of cane, where available, and the hunter could fit a shorter piece of wood or foreshaft into the hollow end of the cane. An arrowhead was tied to this end. The Indians who used a foreshafted arrow found it valuable because when the arrow was shot into an animal, only the main shaft need be removed and another foreshaft attached in order for the hunter to shoot again. If an arrowhead was ruined, the hunter only lost the foreshaft of the arrow and not the entire shaft.

OTHER TOOLS

Indians of Central and Northern California also carried a tool called an **adze** (adz). An adze is made from bone and shell and is used for scraping and chopping. With an adze an Indian could shape a log and hollow it out. Most wood is too hard for this tool so the Indians burned the wood first. The partly burned wood was easier to scrape with this **ingenious** tool. It was used mostly by the Northern California Indians for making boats.

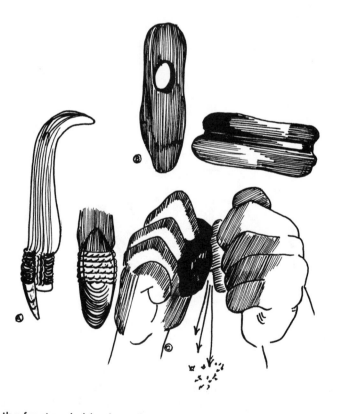

A. This is the front and side view of an adze. A piece of mussel shell was tightly tied to a curved bone. The bone was used as a handle and the shell used for scraping.
B. These are arrow straighteners made of stone.
C. Some Indians struck two pieces of quartz or flint together to make sparks and start a fire.

Arrow straighteners were carried by many California Indians. An arrow straightener is a piece of rock or soapstone that can be heated in a fire. A groove the size of an arrowshaft was chipped into the rock. When the rock was heated, the wooden arrowshaft was moved back and forth in the heated groove. This would straighten out a bent or crooked arrowshaft. Another kind of stone arrow straightener was used. A crooked arrowshaft was pulled through a hole in a heated flat piece of soapstone. Water sprinkled on the wooden arrowshaft caused the wood to steam and the crooked part of the shaft straightened as it cooled.

An important tool for every Indian man was a fire drill. Indians had no matches to start a fire. They used a flat piece of wood with a few holes on one side. The Indians of Northwestern California used cottonwood roots. The holes in the wood were not deep. The Indians twirled a pointed stick on one of the holes until the wood got hotter and hotter. They laid some fine, dry leaves near the hole, and when the wood was very hot, this tinder began to burn. Tinder is very dry and easily catches fire. With the burning tinder they started a larger fire.

NATURAL RESOURCES

Indians settled in areas where there was a good food and water supply as well as fertile lands. They scattered out along the sea coast and in the mountains, valleys and deserts. They loved the land of California and many of them never moved again. The **area** where an Indian was born was usually the area where an Indian died. The Indians were the first **inhabitants** of this state.

The Indians used many **natural resources.** Natural resources are the useful plants, trees, animals, fish, water and minerals that are a part of the land. It was a **bountiful** land and the Indians took care of what nature had given to them. They never wasted or **depleted** a natural resource.

One of the more useful natural resources was a rock called obsidian. Obsidian is a hard, **volcanic** glass that comes in colors of red, white and black; black being the most common. Obsidian is found in volcanic areas, such as Mt. Lassen, Mt. Shasta and Clear Lake. Another type of stone used by the Indians was chert. Chert is a hard stone with a waxlike **luster** and comes in colors of blue, gray, green and red. Both obsidian and chert, as well as other stones such as **flint** or jasper, were used because these stones break with a sharp edge. Since ancient times, Indians all over California had learned to chip these hard stones into blades. Men put these pointed blades on the ends of wooden shafts. They used other blades for knife-like tools to remove skins from animals they had killed. Indian men devoted many patient hours to working these blades called arrowheads. They chipped away at the stone as they hiked to hunting areas or as they sat in friendly groups.

Pieces of flint, chert, obsidian or jasper were skillfully carved into sharp points for knives, choppers or spear points.

TRADE AMONG THE INDIANS

When the Indians traveled, it was for acorn gathering, mesquite gathering, agave gathering and visiting with other tribes. One of the most important reasons for traveling, however, was to trade with other tribes. **Trading** was important to all Indians because through trading they could get goods that were not available in the area where they lived. Some areas of California lacked certain resources, such as good wood for bows, obsidian for arrowheads, salt, cinnabar for coloring, shells or perhaps **soapstone** for bowls and carvings. Trading among the tribes was valuable because it allowed the Indians to gain goods that otherwise they may not have had.

When the Indian traders arrived at a village to trade their goods, they often did not speak the language of the tribe they were to trade with. There were over one hundred native languages spoken in California, but this did not stop the Indians from trading. Indian traders learned to **communicate** with other tribes because someone in the tribe often knew a language that was similar. For example, if you know a few words of Spanish, you could probably understand a few words of Italian or perhaps even French!

The Indians who traded with each other learned to be fair to one another. If a trader made an offer, the other person accepted the offer and did not argue with him. It was important for the traders to have good, honest **reputations** so others would want to trade with them.

The traveling routes that the Indians used went up and down and across the land. These routes had been used for thousands of years. The trails were from six inches to twelve inches wide. Because the Indians used these trails so often, the trails were worn down many inches. Often the trails were lined with stones on each side. All the Indians did their part to keep the trails clear. The trails were sacred to the Indians. Rest spots were marked along the trails where the Indians might stop and rest. Have you noticed that highways of today also have rest stops?

One of these trade routes went along the coast between the mountains and stretched from San Francisco Bay to San Diego Bay. There was another trade route that followed the San Joaquin River through the Central Valley and across the lands of the Yokuts and Wintun Indians. In Southern California routes led across the hot desert. Indians from the Nevada and Arizona tribes used these desert routes to trade with Indians where Los Angeles and San Diego are now located. The routes the Indians used are still in use today. Highways 1, 10, 36, 76, 78, 101, 126, 127, 138, 299, 395, as well as other highways, follow the original Indian trails.

Indians of Southern California, especially the Gabrielino, traded with the coastal island Indians for soapstone. This soft stone was chipped, carved and shaped into bowls. These bowls were traded to many tribes far from the coast. Southern California Indians traded with other tribes for bear grass, bow wood, salt, deerskins, **pumice** stone, soapstone, clam shells, dried fish, jasper points and **asphaltum.**

Hupa Indians in Northern California traded with their neighbors, the Yuroks, who lived on the coast. The Hupa Indians often traded seeds, nuts and deerskins for redwood canoes, dried fish, salty seaweed and bow wood. A Hupa Indian might have traded a bow, a fur quiver and many arrows for a good boat. They might also have exchanged a boat, deerskins, red woodpecker scalps or tools for bows and arrows. Many times, however, the Indians paid for goods with strings of **dentalium** shell money.

Dentalium shells were used as money by some Indians. Dentalium shells come from north of the state of Washington near Vancouver Island. The Hupa and some other Indian tribes considered the dentalium valuable. These shells were shaped like small tusks or teeth. They were more highly valued by the Indians than other common shells such as **limpet, olivella** and **turban** shells. The Northern Indians used only the shells that were 1-7/8 inches or longer for money. Some Indian traders had **tattoos** on their arms so they could measure each shell. The most valuable shell was 2-1/2 inches long. The people decorated these shells with fishskin, snakeskin and tipped them with red feathers. They were wrapped in soft fur such as mink or rabbit or carried in a hand-carved elkhorn case.

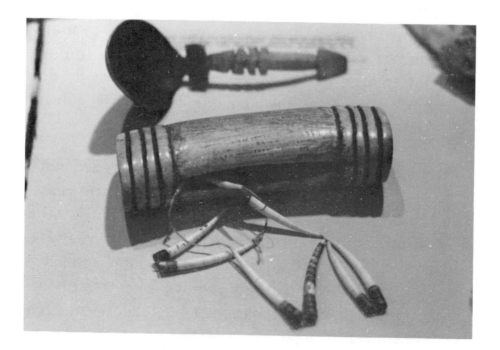

The elkhorn purse was used by the Indians to carry dentalium.

Clam shells were traded by the Indians of the coast. The shells were broken into pieces and each piece was ground on a rough stone until it was a smooth, round **disc.** This took many hours of patient work. Holes were made in the center with a sharp pointed stone and the shells were strung into necklaces or used as money. Indians often used these beads as a sign of wealth.

The Pomo Indians, who lived near Clear Lake, found a stone called **magnesite.** This stone was not very hard and could be ground into small round pieces. When the stone was heated and polished, it turned shades of pink, red or gold. The Pomo Indians strung the magnesite beads with shell beads. These beads were highly prized for trading and often more valuable than dentalium.

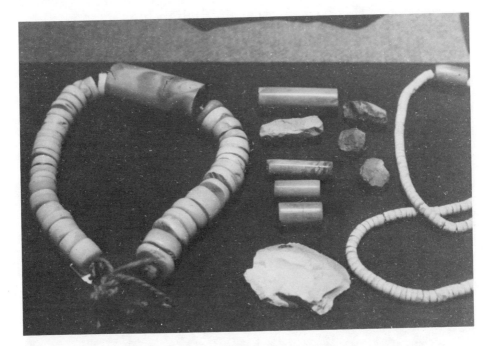

Magnesite and clam shell beads

INTERESTING THOUGHTS

Today, as you travel the busy highways of California, there is little to remind you of the land that the first Indians knew. As your car speeds along the freeways, passing homes, shopping centers and factories, you will have to use your imagination to take you back in time. Imagine the following scene:

> The hillsides are covered with oak trees, deer and elk and the valleys are filled with tules and grassy fields. Trails can be seen winding through the hills and leading to an Indian village in the distance. Indians are walking along the trails carrying trading packs on their backs. You can hear the shouts of excited Indian children racing down the trails to greet visitors. A covey of quail skitters into the dry grass as the children run by. Wisps of smoke from village fires drift and rise above this peaceful scene of Indian life.

The scene that you have just imagined was a part of the Indians' everyday life throughout California—a way of life in harmony with nature—a way of life never to be forgotten!

BACKTRACKING

Can you answer the following questions?

(1) List several belongings for Indian men and women and tell why each was important.

(2) Where did the Indians settle in California? Why did they choose these areas?

(3) What are natural resources? Why were they important to the Indians?

(4) What is obsidian? Why was it used by the Indians?

(5) Why was trade important to an Indian tribe?

(6) Why would an Indian trader want to have a good reputation?

(7) List some things the Southern California Indians might have asked for in exchange for their own trade items?

(8) List some things the Northern California Indians might have asked for in exchange for their own trade items?

(9) What is dentalium and why was it highly prized among the Indians?

(10) What other types of shells or stones were prized as exchange items?

*For Wise Eagles: The Mojave Indians probably did more trading with other tribes than any other California tribe. Why do you think this was so?

*For Wise Eagles: Look up the word petroglyphs in your dictionary or encyclopedia.
What does it mean?
It has been noted that petroglyphs were commonly used along trade routes.
What significance would they have had?

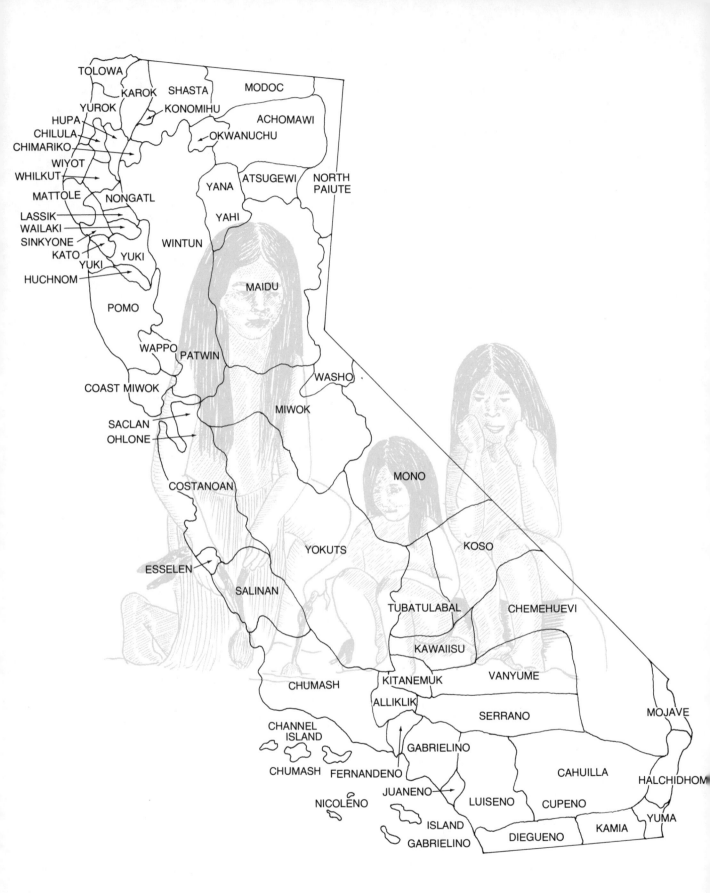

CHAPTER THREE
NATURE'S NOURISHMENT

SEEDS, ROOTS AND PLANTS

THE FIRST ECOLOGISTS

Nature's **nourishment** for the California Indians was a varied diet of deer, small animals, birds, fish, native plants and insects. The Indians gathered bulbs and tender plant shoots in the spring, seeds in the summer, acorns in the fall and mushrooms in the winter. During the winter months, the diet of the Indians consisted mainly of dried meat, acorns, dried vegetables, seeds and nuts. The Indians also traded with other Indian groups for such things as salt, dried or fresh shellfish and **pinyon (pine)** nuts. Foods were gathered for daily use, but most of the food was dried and stored for the winter. Thus, nature provided the Indians with year-round nourishment.

Indians were the first **ecologists.** They made use of everything on the land and particular use of the native plants. When the Indians used a wild plant, they usually found a use for every part of the plant. Among all the California Indians, the woman was the gatherer of all plant foods. In today's society she would be considered an expert **botanist**! In her **explorations** for food for herself and family, she made tests with her teeth and stomach on every grass, stalk, fruit, root and seed that she could find. She examined all plant foods carefully because she knew that she was responsible for the plant food needs of her entire family. If certain plants were not available during times of **drought,** the Indian woman had to know about other plants that could be **substituted.** She knew she had to gather the seeds and plants as well as prepare them for eating and storing. Can you imagine the **responsibility** and **patience** an Indian woman must have had to have in order to accomplish this **monumental** task?

Indian women gathered nuts and berries in the summer and fall. They had to watch out for "visitors" because the Indians weren't the only ones who liked these treats!

THE MIGHTY OAK

Now, let's take a closer look at one of the main sources of food for the California Indians. Oak trees grew in most of California and the seed of the oak tree, called the **acorn,** provided most of the food for the California Indians. There were as many as fourteen kinds of oaks growing in all of California and about eight of these varieties are found in the southern part of the state. All of the acorns are **edible,** but some are better than others. Acorns contain starch, oil, sugar and **citric** acid. Some are sweet, but many are bitter because they contain **tannic** acid.

There are basically two groups of oak trees in North America—the white oaks and the black or red oaks. The acorns of the white oaks are sweeter, make better eating and are smooth inside. The black oak acorns are nearly always bitter and are furry inside. The white oak is found throughout the state, on the plains, in the foothills and somewhat higher in the mountains of Southern California.

GATHERING ACORNS

In the fall or autumn of the year, the Indians gathered acorns. The men and boys climbed the oak trees and knocked the acorns to the ground. The women and children gathered the acorns in baskets. Also, long sticks were used to knock acorns from the trees. People today still use long sticks to knock walnuts, almonds or other types of nuts from the trees. Indian families camped by the oak groves during the harvesting season. Sometimes, while they were camped in the oak groves, the men would hunt and the women would pound the acorns into meal. It was easier to carry acorn meal back to the villages than it was to carry burden baskets of whole acorns. **Mortars** and **pestles** were used for pounding the acorns into meal. These stone tools were often left at the oak

groves from year to year. Oak groves were owned by
Indian tribes and trees within the grove were owned
by Indian families. If a tree did not produce, the family
leader would ask another family leader, whose trees
had produced, if he could gather acorns from his trees.

Family groups worked together to collect acorns.

STORING ACORNS

Most of the acorns that were gathered in the fall were stored for the winter. The Indians built storehouses called **granaries** for the acorns. Here the acorns would be safe from **rodents** and birds. One type of granary was built off the ground, supported by a framework of small poles. The poles were usually covered with sticky **pitch** to prevent the rodents from entering. The granary itself was made of tule or brush and often covered at the top with an animal skin to keep out moisture. In high altitudes granaries were made doubly thick to withstand snow. The Indians of the south wove granaries from willow or other plant materials and placed them on pole-like legs or on top of high **boulders.** When an Indian woman wanted some acorns from the granary, she would pull apart the woven twigs near the base of the granary, making a small hole. When she had enough acorns, she would push the twigs back in place and close the hole. If a granary was more tightly woven, the woman would lift a tule or skin cover at the top to reach the acorns.

Other tribes, such as the Northern Maidu, stored extra acorns in holes dug into the sides of hills and lined the holes with pine needles. After the holes were filled, the acorns were covered with **cedar** bark and dirt. A long stick was also pounded into the ground to mark the location of the hole.

This type of granary was used by some of the Indians of Southern California.

There are more than 1200 holes in these rocks at Chaw-se State Park. Indian women sat talking together as they ground their acorns into meal.

PREPARING ACORNS

Indian women prepared the acorns for eating. The outer shells of the acorns were removed by breaking the shells with a firm tap from a hammerstone. The thin skins on the acorns were **winnowed** off. The women used a stone mortar and stone pestle to pound the acorn **kernels** into meal. Sometimes the women sat on large boulders and pounded the acorns in a hole in the rock. In some areas today you can still see where Indian women once pounded acorns.

This Indian woman is using a winnowing basket. A winnowing basket is a flat, shallow basket used to separate the unneeded skin-like covering of the acorn from the kernel of the acorn. The winnowing basket was used to toss the acorn kernels into the air. As the acorns were tossed, the wind blew away the unneeded coverings from the acorns. Winnowing the coverings from the acorn kernels took much time.

All kinds of nuts and seeds that grew in California were gathered by the Indians. The women would sit and pound the nuts and grains, using a stone pestle and mortar. Some women used a bottomless basket set on a flat stone. In Southern California a woman might attach her bottomless basket to a round stone with asphaltum. Other women sat on large boulders and pounded their seeds in the hollows of the boulder. Today, in many parts of California, you can still see where Indian women of the past pounded seeds and acorns on the boulders.

As the Indian woman pounded in the mortar, the sides of the bottomless baskets kept the meal from flying out. Many Indians used mortars and pestles to pound acorns and seeds. Some of these grinding tools might still be found today. Mortars and pestles may be seen in museums. Some of these grinding rocks have a black ring around them. This indicates that a bottomless basket was attached with asphaltum. What do you notice about the acorns in this mortar?

The acorn meal had a bitter taste due to the natural tannic acid. This acid had to be taken out before the acorn meal could be used for food. The Indian women had ways to remove this bad taste. Some women made a little hollow in clean, hard packed sand by the side of a stream. In some mountain areas, the women lined this hollow with pine needles. The acorn meal was spread on the pine needles and fir boughs were placed across the acorn meal. Water was poured gently over the meal and allowed to trickle through to the sand. The water carried the tannic acid into the sand and left the acorn meal with a pleasant taste. If warm water was poured over the meal, it took less time to remove the tannic acid. When the sand had settled, the women would **skim** off the acorn meal and it was then ready to be used for soup or mush or acorn patties.

Another way Indian women **leached** the tannic acid from the acorn meal was to place the meal in a loosely woven leaching basket and use a layer of grass or leaves to line the basket. This would keep the meal from being washed away. Then, the same process of pouring warm or cold water over the meal was followed. Leaching tannic acid from acorn meal often took several hours, depending on the type of acorn used.

An Indian woman is removing the bitter tannic acid from the acorn meal before using it to make bread.

An Indian woman had her digging stick, her stirring paddles and looped sticks. This woman is using her looped stick to put a hot rock into a basket of corn mush. The rock will heat the acorn mush and cook it.

When the acorn meal was ready, the women mixed it with water in a **watertight** basket. Then the meal was cooked by using a looped stick to place clean, hot stones into the cooking basket. The warmth from the heated stones cooked the water and acorn meal into a mush. The mush was stirred constantly to keep the hot rocks from burning the bottom of the basket. The rocks were then removed and the mush was ready to eat. These cooking stones were special stones, because the Indians had to use a certain rock that would not break or shatter when heated. These types of rocks are called **igneous.** An igneous rock is formed as **volcanic magma** or **lava** is cooled. The Indian women carefully cleaned the cooking stones before and after each use. In the desert areas, pottery bowls were used directly over the fire to cook the acorn mush. Along the coast, soapstone bowls were used by the Indians.

People today are called good cooks if the food they prepare is tasty and appealing to the eye. You might think an Indian woman had little chance to show her cooking skills due to the basic diet of acorns. But the skill and care shown by an Indian woman in pounding and preparing acorns often gave her a reputation as a good or bad cook. A good cook was imaginative in adding nuts or berries to her acorn meal. If the acorn meal was bitter, unappealing to the eye or if the mortars and pestles used were not kept clean, the Indian woman was known as a poor cook.

*   *   *   *   *

A LEGEND FROM NORTHERN CALIFORNIA

The following legend is called "The Acorn Maidens". It is told by the Indians of Northern California.

*THE ACORN MAIDENS

"It is said that once acorns were Yassaras (spirits). Life Givers came and told them, 'You are going to go. You must all have nice hats, but you must weave them.'

When they started to weave their hats, they said, 'We must all wear good looking hats.'

Then suddenly, Life Giver told them, 'You better go. Human is being raised.'

*The legend, "The Acorn Maidens", is quoted exactly as it is printed in the Humboldt County Office of Education N.I.C.E. program.

Black Oak Acorn had not finished her hat. She picked up her big pole basket. And Tan Oak Acorn did not clean her hat, and the uneven straw ends stuck out the side of her basket, so she just wore it wrong side out when she finished it.

The Post Oak Acorn just finished her hat out good. She finished and cleaned it well.

Then Tan Oak Acorn said, 'Wouldn't I be the best acorn soup though my hat is not cleaned?'

Then they went. They spilled (from the heavens) into Human's place. Then they said, 'Human will spoon us up. They were Yassaras (spirits) too, but they were heavenly Yassaras.'

They shut their eyes and then turned their faces into their hats when they came to this earth here. That is the way the acorns did.

Tan Oak Acorn began to wish bad luck toward Post Oak Acorn and Maul Oak Acorn just because they had nice hats. She was jealous of them. They, in turn, wished her to be black.

Nobody likes to eat Post Oak Acorn and Maul Oak Acorn does not taste good either. Their soups are black and Maul Oak Acorn is too hard to pound.

They were all painted when they first spilled down. Black Oak Acorn was striped. When one picks it up off the ground nowadays, it is still striped.

Tan Oak Acorn was also all striped, but she did not paint herself much because she was mad. Because, she said, 'My hat is not finished.'

When they spilled down, they turned their faces into their hats. And nowadays, they still have their faces inside their hats."

* * * * *

There were other important uses of the oak tree. Wood from this tree was very useful in making a hot, long-lasting fire and considered one of the best materials for making wooden mortars. Oak wood and bark were burned and used in medicines. The oak gall, a fungus that sometimes grows on the oak tree, was pounded into a powder and used as a wash for the eyes or open sores. It was also mixed with deer brains, cooked and used for tanning hides.

AGAVE OR CENTURY PLANT

Acorns were the main **staple** food for the Indians throughout California. In Southern California, however, the Indians used other important plant sources, one of them being **agave,** also called mescal or century plant.

Three parts of the agave were used—the flower, the leaves and the stalk. The flowers of the agave plant were gathered and boiled a few minutes to remove the bitter taste. They were eaten or dried for later use. The dried flowers could be stored for as long as five years. When the Indian family was ready to use the dried flowers, they were reheated and "plumped-up" in warm water. As the Indians picked the flowers, they also could pick the leaves. The leaves were best when picked in the fall to spring months because they were plump and juicy. The leaves were baked and eaten or dried for later use. The stalk of the agave was the most prized part of the plant. The stalk was best before it started to flower. When the stalk started to flower, it became **fibrous** and was not as tasty. Stalks were roasted in underground pits. The roasted stalks were eaten or pounded into small patties and sun dried. These patties were stored for later use.

Indians could harvest agave in April and May, but the best time was in November and December. Harvesting the agave involved cutting down the whole plant—flowers, leaves and stalks. The agave plant, however, is much like a banana tree. Even though most of the plant is destroyed in harvesting, it will still send out small, new, young shoots that will root and grow into new plants. As the agave **matured,** the plants had to be carefully watched because animals liked to nibble the sweet, **succulent** leaves.

The thorns of the agave were used for tattooing and the fibers from the pounded leaves were used for sandals, nets, mats, snares, slings and bowstrings.

Agave gathering areas were owned by families, just like some families owned acorn groves. Harvesting the broad flat cactus-like leaves was usually a man's job.

MESQUITE, ANOTHER IMPORTANT BASIC FOOD

Another main food source for Southern California Indians was the **mesquite.** These trees and shrubs grew in groves and like the agave and acorn, were useful in many ways. The Indians ate the blossoms in the spring, the green bean pods in the summer and the dried pods in the fall. The flowers were picked and boiled before eating. Sometimes, they were made into tea. The green bean pods were crushed in mortars made of mesquite wood. A stone pestle was used to pound the pods. The Cahuilla people made a refreshing summer drink by adding water to the crushed pods. This drink was stored in **ollas.** The dried pods, gathered in autumn, were eaten soon after picking or pounded into meal. Water was added to the meal. Later, when the meal had dried, it was formed into patties or cakes. The mesquite cakes were stored for future use and were excellent for traders or hunters to take with them on long journeys.

Mesquite wood made good hot, long burning fires and the wood was also used for bows. The **framework** of some desert homes was made from mesquite boughs and the boughs were also used for holding up large granaries. The thicker pieces of wood were made into mortars for pounding mesquite seeds into meal. The Yuma Indians made a mush or soup from the mesquite meal and used it as part of their marriage ceremonies while other desert Indians made a kind of candy from the sweet **gum** or pitch of the mesquite.

Mesquite is a thick growing tree or shrub. At harvest time the Indians cut back or snapped off branches of the mesquite so that Indian children could crawl under the bushes and gather the bean pods. A favorite hiding place for small game animals, such as rabbits, was under the shelter of the mesquite. While Indian women and children gathered the bean pods, the men would hunt these small animals.

PINE NUTS

The men did the hunting and fishing and the women gathered seeds, roots, berries and nuts. Pine nuts were gathered and prized by tribes throughout California. Pine nuts were collected in the fall and Indian families made long journeys into the mountains to gather them. The Indians knocked the pinecones from the pine trees and removed the nuts from the pinecones. When pine nuts were collected, a winnowing basket was used to separate the nuts from small twigs or sticks. The nuts were then roasted by putting them in a basket with hot coals. The basket and nuts were shaken so that the coals would not burn the basket and the nuts were well roasted. Then the shells were cracked with a stone. Again the winnowing basket was used to separate the nutmeats from the shells. The nutmeats were roasted one more time and once again the winnowing basket was used to separate the nutmeats from the ashes left by the hot coals. Often an Indian woman said a silent prayer to the winds to help her with the winnowing.

Pine nuts were also eaten raw, boiled into a mush or ground and made into cakes. Tiny babies were often fed a thin mush made from pine nuts. Pine nuts are rich in protein and fat and were a welcome addition to the Indian's diet.

* * * * *

A PAIUTE PRAYER

*Paiute Pinenut Prayer

"When we come to a pinenut place we talk to the ground and mountain and everything. We ask to feel good and strong. We ask for cool breezes to sleep at night. The pinenuts belong to the mountain so we ask the mountain for some of its pinenuts to take home and eat. The water is the mountain's juice. It comes out of the mountain, so we ask the mountain for some of its juice to make us feel good and happy. Just the old people do this. The young people don't care; they just walk on the mountain anyhow."

* * * * *

*The poem, "Paiute Pinenut Prayer", is quoted exactly as it is printed in the book entitled **Survival Arts of the Primitive Paiutes** by Margaret M. Wheat, published by the University of Nevada Press.

HARVEST TIMES

Harvesting seasons for acorns, agave, mesquite and pine nuts were special occasions for the Indians. Friends and relatives who had not seen each other for several months, camped side by side and listened to each other's stories of births, deaths, marriages and other recent happenings among the tribes. These times also were **courting** times for young men and women.

SOME INDIANS PLANTED CROPS

Most of the California Indians did not grow green vegetables, but they did have green plants in their diet. They gathered nettle, wild onions, bracken greens, Indian or Miner's lettuce and many other green plants. Most of the Indians did not grow crops because they were skilled gatherers of nature's gifts that grew **abundantly** in all of California. The Indian women gathered seeds, roots, plants, flowers—every type of plant that could be used as food. What they did not eat immediately, they dried and stored for winter use. The Indians respected nature and never took more than their family or tribes could use. There is evidence, however, that Indians in parts of Southern California grew crops long before white men came. The Indians along the Colorado River grew squash and pumpkin and the overflow from the river watered their crops. The squash and pumpkin were boiled or roasted in a fire and the seeds were sun-dried for winter use.

Few tribes planted crops, but many tribes practiced burning the fields and meadows. The Indians knew that burning would remove unnecessary plants or brush on the land. The ashes from the burning enriched the soil so that the following season the young plants grew stronger. The Indians learned about burning by observing nature at work. When lightning caused a fire and the land was burned, the Indians noticed that the following season's plant growth was more **productive** than usual. And so, the Indians learned that by controlled burning of grasslands, they could look forward to a more abundant food supply.

OTHER NATIVE PLANTS
USED BY THE INDIANS

On the following pages, you will find pictures, descriptions and uses of some native plants used by the California Indians. When you come to the conclusion of each plant description, you will notice how, today, we use these same plants that the Indians discovered and put to use long before the white man came.

Before you read about the following plants used by the Indians, you should understand that eating any of the plants without properly identifying them could lead to stomach disorders. Never eat any plant without first checking with a knowledgeable person.

* * * * *

ANGELICA

DESCRIPTION

This stout plant grows one to four feet high and is related to the celery family. The leaf stalks have leaves in groups of three.

HABITAT

Angelica grows on the plains and high in the mountains.

INDIAN USES

The root is dried, used in pipes and smoked in ceremonies. The dried root is used on cuts and sores and sometimes brewed into a strong tea for people who were very ill. Poultices were made from this plant and used for rheumatic pains.

USES TODAY

Angelica is still used in some Indian ceremonies.

ARROWHEAD
TULE POTATO

DESCRIPTION

The Arrowhead plant stands one to three feet in height. It has long arrow shaped leaves with flowers that come from the top of the stem and stand higher than the leaves. The flowers are white with gold or green centers.

HABITAT

This plant grows in wet marshy areas, ponds and fresh water river edges.

INDIAN USES

The roots were eaten raw, roasted or boiled.

USES TODAY

The roots make excellent outdoorsman food for they are used just like a potato.

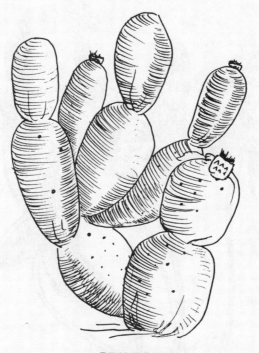

BEAVERTAIL
PRICKLY PEAR

DESCRIPTION

The Beavertail is a cactus with flat, fleshy joints or pads. It grows in clumps with fine short spines. Large, waxy flowers appear on the cactus in the spring. The fruit that forms on the cactus is reddish, pear shaped and very juicy.

HABITAT

This cactus grows in the desert areas of Southern California.

INDIAN USES

The large fleshy joints or pads were split and scraped and used as a wet dressing to help reduce swelling and deaden the pain from bites or wounds. The fruit and young fleshy joints (with the spines removed) were dried in the sun, then boiled and eaten. The young fruits were also cooked in stone lined pits.

USES TODAY

The fruit can be eaten raw or made into jelly or pickles. The young fleshy joints or pads are cooked and used as a vegetable.

BARBERRY
OREGON GRAPE

DESCRIPTION

The Barberry is a tall bush with bright green crisp leaves. It has yellow flowers that blossom in the spring.

HABITAT

The Barberry is found on the wooded slopes of California.

INDIAN USES

The roots and bark were used to heal ulcers and sores, and were also used to treat heartburn and rheumatism. The bark and roots were made into a yellow dye.

USES TODAY

Tea is made from the roots and used as a diuretic and laxative.

BEARGRASS

DESCRIPTION

Beargrass has long slender leaves growing upward from the bulb with small white flowers that form clusters. The leaves and stalk are very slippery. Beargrass is also called Bear Lily, Pine Lily or Elk Grass.

HABITAT

The plant grows on mountain slopes and high open forests of Northern California. It grows at higher altitudes—6000 feet and over.

INDIAN USES

Parts of the plant were dried and bleached and the fibers were used for white patterns in baskets.

USES TODAY

Fibers from the plant are used in basket making today.

BRACKEN FERN

DESCRIPTION

The Bracken Fern grows one to four feet high and toothlike leaves grow from the stalks.

HABITAT

The ferns grow in ponds, streams, open woods and meadows.

INDIAN USES

The starchy root was boiled and eaten. In the spring the young tender curled tips were used as a green vegetable.

USES TODAY

In Siberia the roots are brewed in ale and mixed with malt to form a beverage. In Europe a tea is made from the plant and used as an astringent in preparing chamois leather. The Japanese use Bracken Fern in soup.

CALIFORNIA BAY
CALIFORNIA LAUREL

DESCRIPTION

The California Bay tree grows fifty to one hundred feet high. It has dark green leaves that give off a strong odor when crushed. The flowers are greenish yellow. The small round nuts turn dark purple.

HABITAT

These trees are found along streamsides and in woodlands.

INDIAN USES

The leaves were used in many types of medicines. They were bound to the forehead or placed in the nostril to cure headaches. The leaves were also bound around the stomach to cure stomach aches. The leaves were used as a flea repellent or sometimes burned in the home when someone had a cold. The nuts were roasted, cracked and pounded into small cakes.

USES TODAY

The leaves are placed in chicken houses to prevent lice, and when hung with garlic to dry, they prevent molding. The leaves are also used in cooking.

CAMAS

DESCRIPTION

The stalk of the Camas plant grows two feet high with small dark blue blossoms.

HABITAT

The Camas grows in moist ground and is found in meadows and among pine forests.

INDIAN USES

Camas bulbs were baked, boiled or pounded into meal. The cooked bulbs were pressed into thick brown cakes or sometimes boiled down into a thick molasses.

USES TODAY

Bulbs are cooked and made into pies.

CASCARA TREE OR SHRUB

DESCRIPTION

Cascara trees or shrubs have smooth gray, brownish bark, dark green oblong shaped leaves and round black berries.

HABITAT

These trees grow in Northwestern California below 5000 feet.

INDIAN USES

The bark was peeled, dried and used as a laxative.

USES TODAY

Cascara is used as a natural laxative in medicine today and can be found in health food stores. The flexible stems are used in wicker furniture.

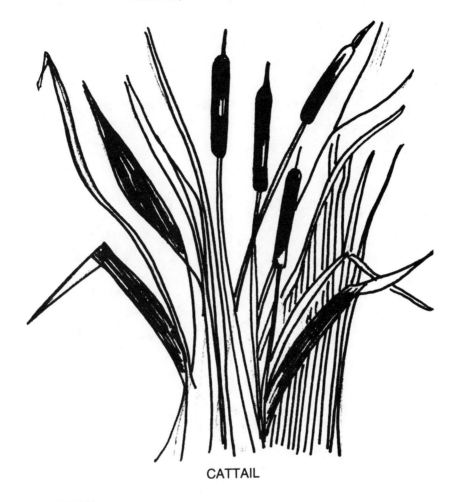

CATTAIL

DESCRIPTION

Cattail plants are three to seven feet tall with long slender leaves and sausage shaped catkins.

HABITAT

Cattails are found in ponds, streams and marshlands of California.

INDIAN USES

The roots were eaten raw or roasted and the young roots were considered a delicacy. The pollen from the catkin was mixed with water and made into little cakes for bread. Some parts of the cattail were used as diaper material for young babies.

USES TODAY

The tender inner leaves are gathered and eaten as a snack or put in salad.

CEANOTHUS

DESCRIPTION

The Ceanothus is a small tree or shrub, two to twenty feet high. It is evergreen with tiny leaves. The flowers bloom white to blue and have a spicy odor.

HABITAT

The Ceanothus is found on open slopes, woodlands and coastal areas throughout California.

INDIAN USES

The bark and roots were brewed as a tea and used as a tonic, while the leaves were sometimes smoked as tobacco. The Ceanothus seeds were eaten. The red roots gave a red dye, and the blossoms were rubbed on the skin as a wash.

USES TODAY

Parts of the plants are used in many medicines—blood coagulant, stimulant for getting rid of mucous and a liver and spleen medicine.

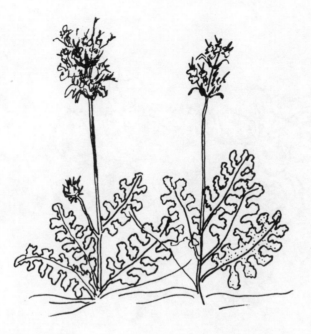

CHIA

DESCRIPTION

The Chia plant grows three to fifteen feet high with small blue flowers and gray green leaves. The brown stalks have clusters at the top much like dried sunflower heads.

HABITAT

Chia grows in much of California below 4000 feet. It can be found in woodlands and grasslands.

INDIAN USES

The Indians gathered the nutritional seeds and ground them to be cooked later as mush or soup. One teaspoon of the dried seeds would give an Indian enough energy for 24 hours! A strong tea made from parts of the plant was used as a stomach medicine or to relieve soreness or infection of the eyes. Seeds were sometimes stirred into the water to neutralize the alkaline water of the desert water holes.

USES TODAY

The seeds are sold in health food stores and are sprouted and used in salads or sandwiches. The seeds can also be made into a tea or stirred into lemonade to make a refreshing drink.

FREMONTIA

DESCRIPTION

The Fremontia is a scraggly growing shrub or tree growing from six to twenty feet tall. The leathery dark green leaves are fuzzy underneath and yellow, saucerlike flowers grow in May and June. The seed capsules are covered with bristly, rust colored hairs.

HABITAT

The Fremontia grows throughout California on hillsides and in dry areas.

INDIAN USES

The fiber from the bark was sometimes twisted into string and the smaller branches were used for making bows and arrows. The slippery inner bark was used for poultices. Sometimes the bark was brewed into a tea for irritations of the throat.

USES TODAY

The Fremontia is used in drought areas and along highways as a decorative plant.

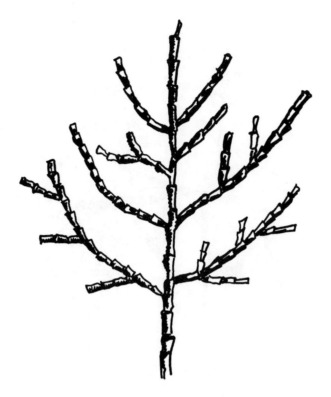

GLASSWORT
SALTWORT

DESCRIPTION

Glasswort is a fleshy herb with jointed branched stems. It has no leaves. In the summer the stems are bright shiny green and in the autumn the stems are yellow-orange and red.

HABITAT

This plant grows in salt marshes along the coast line.

INDIAN USES

The Indians ate Glasswort raw. They dried it and traded it.

USES TODAY

Glasswort can be added to salad or made into pickles.

INDIAN LETTUCE
MINER'S LETTUCE

DESCRIPTION

This dainty looking plant grows six to twelve inches tall. The leaves are a roundish shape and encircle the stem. Above the stem, growing out of the center of the leaf, are clusters of pink or white flowers.

HABITAT

Indian Lettuce is found in mountain and coastal pine forests as well as oak woodlands.

INDIAN USES

The tender leaves were eaten green or cooked. A tea was made and used as a laxative. Some Placer County Indians picked the plants and placed them near a red ant nest. They let the ants crawl over the leaves and then shook the plants clean. A residue tasting like a vinegar salad dressing would remain!

USES TODAY

The greens are picked and used in salads.

INDIAN SOAP PLANT

DESCRIPTION

The Indian Soap Plant (Amole) grows two to three feet tall with long narrow fluted leaves. The flowers have white petals with green veins. The fiber covered bulb grows underground.

HABITAT

The Indian Soap Plant can be found growing on hillsides, in valleys and woodlands, grasslands and by streams.

INDIAN USES

Some Indians used the crushed bulb of the soap plant to stupify fish in rivers and streams. Rope and small brushes were made from the brown outer fibers of the bulb. The inner part of the soap root was made into a paste and used on skin irritations. The crushed bulb was used as a shampoo and when baked the bulb was edible. The gluey substance that oozed from the bulb during baking was used by the Indians for gluing feathers to arrow shafts.

USES TODAY

The fibers are used as whisk brooms.

JIMSON WEED

DESCRIPTION

Jimson Weed is a beautiful but very poisonous plant. It has bright green leaves and long bell-shaped white flowers.

HABITAT

Jimson Weed grows in dry places over most of Southern California and as far north as the Sacramento Valley.

INDIAN USES

A brew was made from the crushed seeds and roots which was used in special ceremonies. The leaves were smoked by most of the tribes in the south. The crushed plant could be used on bruises, swellings and bites.

USES TODAY

The plant is used for medicinal purposes as a prescribed drug.

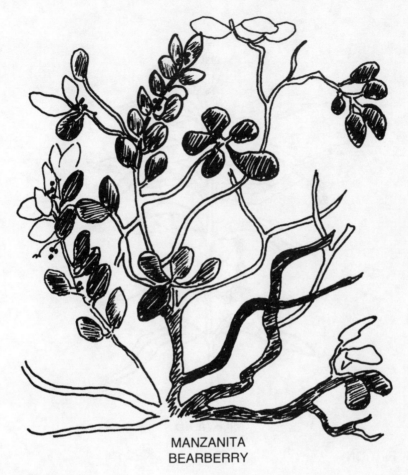

MANZANITA
BEARBERRY

DESCRIPTION

This shrubby evergreen plant has small dark green leaves and reddish brown bark. It has tiny red berries from June to late fall.

HABITAT

Manzanita grows in oak woodlands and in pine forests.

INDIAN USES

The Indians ate the berries raw or dried them for winter use. They sometimes crushed the ripe berries and mixed them with water for a refreshing drink or made them into a thick jellylike mush. The leaves were made into a tea for curing diarrhea. Leaves were sometimes mixed with tobacco for smoking.

USES TODAY

The berries are made into tea or cider.

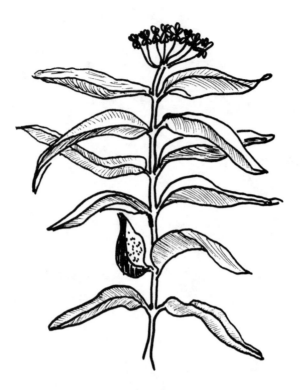

MILKWEED

DESCRIPTION

Milkweed is a tall slender plant two to five feet tall with long narrow leaves. The stems have a milky juice when crushed.

HABITAT

This plant is found throughout California in fields, meadows and woodlands.

INDIAN USES

The Indians removed and dried the outer fibers from the stalk. These fibers were made into string and fishnets. The milky juice from the plant was used for cuts, wounds, tattooing and warts and sometimes hardened and used for chewing gum. The young leaves were used as greens and the roots were boiled for eating.

USES TODAY

The young shoots and buds from the milkweed are cooked or eaten raw in salads. Sometimes the milky juice from this plant is used to cure warts.

NETTLE

DESCRIPTION

Nettle grows from two inches to seven feet tall. The leaves grow opposite one another on a single stalk. The leaves are oblong with a heart shaped base and serrated edges. The older stalks and the underpart of leaves have stinging bristles filled with fluid.

HABITAT

These plants are found throughout California in meadows, fields and woodlands.

INDIAN USES

The young nettles that did not have stinging bristles were gathered and boiled or eaten raw. The young nettles are rich in vitamins and minerals. Parts of the plant were brewed into a tea and used for chest colds and internal pains. Fibers from the plant were woven into cord and thread.

USES TODAY

The young greens are eaten raw in salads or cooked as a vegetable. The fiber is used in material, cording or paper.

SEAWEED (BROWN KELP)

DESCRIPTION

Brown or Red Algae, also known as Kelp, can grow as long as two hundred feet. The Red Algae has fine mosslike leaves and the Brown Algae has wide coarse leaves.

HABITAT

These seaweeds grow in the sea along the coast of California.

INDIAN USES

The Indians gathered and dried the seaweed for use in cooking. It was a valuable trade item because it contained salt.

USES TODAY

Giant Kelp is harvested to make fertilizers and explosives. Chemists extract a large amount of iodine and algin from kelp. Algin is important because it can hold liquids together and is used in milk, ice cream, salad dressing, chocolate and aspirin. Kelp is also dried and eaten.

WILD GRAPE

DESCRIPTION

Wild grape is a vine that grows five to sixty feet long. It bears small clusters of fruit, has large green leaves and curly tendrils. The flowers are small and greenish white.

HABITAT

The Wild Grape is found in moist, fertile ground throughout California along streams, canyons and in woodlands.

INDIAN USES

The Indians sometimes used the wiry branches in baskets and for tying things together. The fruit was eaten fresh or dried and stored for winter use. The Indians ate the leaves and young tender green shoots. Sometimes the leaves were used as a poultice for snakebites.

USES TODAY

Fresh fruit is used for eating, dried for raisins, boiled for jelly and crushed and fermented for wine. The young leaves are used in cooking.

WILD ONION

DESCRIPTION

The Wild Onion has green, slender tubular leaves and stems. The onion bulb grows below ground and has a distinct strong odor. The flowers grow in umbrella shaped clusters of pink and white.

HABITAT

Wild Onion is found in moist ground throughout the west near streams, marshlands and meadows.

INDIAN USES

The Indian ate the wild onion bulbs raw or roasted. They dried and tied the onions into bundles for winter use. The whole plant was used as an insect repellent by rubbing it on the body and sometimes the bulb was pounded into pulp, mixed with animal fat and used on snakebites.

USES TODAY

Onions are roasted, boiled, baked and eaten raw. They are made into cough syrup and sometimes poultices are made from them.

WILD ROSE

DESCRIPTION

The Wild Rose is a scraggly plant that grows three to six feet high. It has pretty pink blossoms. A rose hip (seedpod) forms beneath each blossom.

HABITAT

The Wild Rose is found near streams and rivers.

INDIAN USES

The Indians brewed a tea from the rose hips. The older wood was used for arrow shafts.

USES TODAY

The rose hips are an excellent source of vitamin C and may be found in health food stores. They may be eaten raw or made into tea. The hips are also ground and used in vitamin pills. The rose petals are used raw in salads.

WILD TOBACCO

DESCRIPTION

Tobacco is an herb that grows from one foot to five feet tall. The small, narrow leaves have a strong odor and are poisonous. The trumpet shaped flowers are white to greenish white.

HABITAT

Tobacco grows thoughout a large part of California in washes, dry plains and open valleys. It grows below 8000 feet.

INDIAN USES

The Indians dried and smoked the leaves for ceremonies. The leaves were sometimes crushed and made into poultices for bites and cuts.

USES TODAY

Wild Tobacco leaves are dried and smoked.

WILLOW

DESCRIPTION

Willow trees and bushes come in many varieties. Salix willows have long green dark pointed leaves and grow twenty to thirty feet in height.

HABITAT

This tree is found throughout California near streams and in other moist areas.

INDIAN USES

The Indian women gathered parts of the willow for basket making. Some tribes used the pliable wood for bows. Willow wood was used for frames of homes. Fiber from the bark of the willow was used for nets and clothing. The bark was made into a tea to relieve headache, fever, aches and pains of rheumatism. Some varieties of willow produced seedpods that could be eaten.

USES TODAY

Salicylic acid is extracted from the willow and used in many medicines, especially aspirin.

YERBA SANTA

DESCRIPTION

Yerba Santa is a shrub that grows two feet to eight feet tall. The leaves have a shiny surface but are fuzzy underneath. The dark lavender to white flowers grow in clusters on tiny stalks.

HABITAT

Yerba Santa grows throughout California on dry rocky slopes and in pine forests.

INDIAN USES

The leaves were boiled in a tea for many different ailments such as coughs, colds, sore throats and rheumatism. The crushed leaves were put on arms and legs to relieve pain. The leaves were sometimes chewed as a thirst quencher.

USES TODAY

The dried leaves are brewed for tea.

YUCCA

DESCRIPTION

Yucca is a tall shrub that grows to the height of eighteen feet. It has thickly clustered sharply pointed leaves. The bell-shaped flowers grow on a long stalk.

HABITAT

Yucca is found near desert scrub, chaparral or brush.

INDIAN USES

The flowers, stalks and fruits were eaten by the Indians. The roots were used as soap and the fibers from the plant were used to make brushes. The Yucca was among the most valuable plants used by Southern California Indians.

USES TODAY

The fibers from the plant can be made into burlap, twine and rope. The root is used in commercial shampoos. The Yucca is a natural food remedy for arthritis. The fruits and flowers are used in cooking.

INTERESTING THOUGHTS

Now that you have read about some of the native plants that the California Indians used, you may wish to ask your grandparents or great-grandparents about some of these plants. Perhaps your grandparents might know of other plants that were used for food, such as wild mustard greens or curly dock or clover. Plants such as these just mentioned were brought to America by the first Europeans and the Indians of California soon learned to put them to use.

As a child, your grandparents may remember having a parent apply a mustard plaster to their chests when they had a bad cold. Thick onion syrup was given for coughs. Thick, sweet cascara bark was chewed as a laxative and is still used today in many types of medicines.

The Indians knew the use of every plant, seed and root growing in California. Their supermarkets were in their backyards and they valued every growing thing that the Great Spirit had created for them.

BACKTRACKING

Can you answer the following questions?

(1) Name some of the major sources of food for the Indians.

(2) How were acorns gathered and prepared for eating and storage?

(3) What Indian groups grew crops of vegetables? Why did they do so—why not other Indian groups?

(4) Name two native plants and their medicinal uses. What medicine could you use today that would have the same medicinal properties?

(5) Why were rose hips and Camas plants so popular with the Indians?

(6) Name three native plants that you can find in your neighborhood. How did the Indians use these plants?

*For Wise Eagles: How do you think the Indians discovered uses for the native plants?

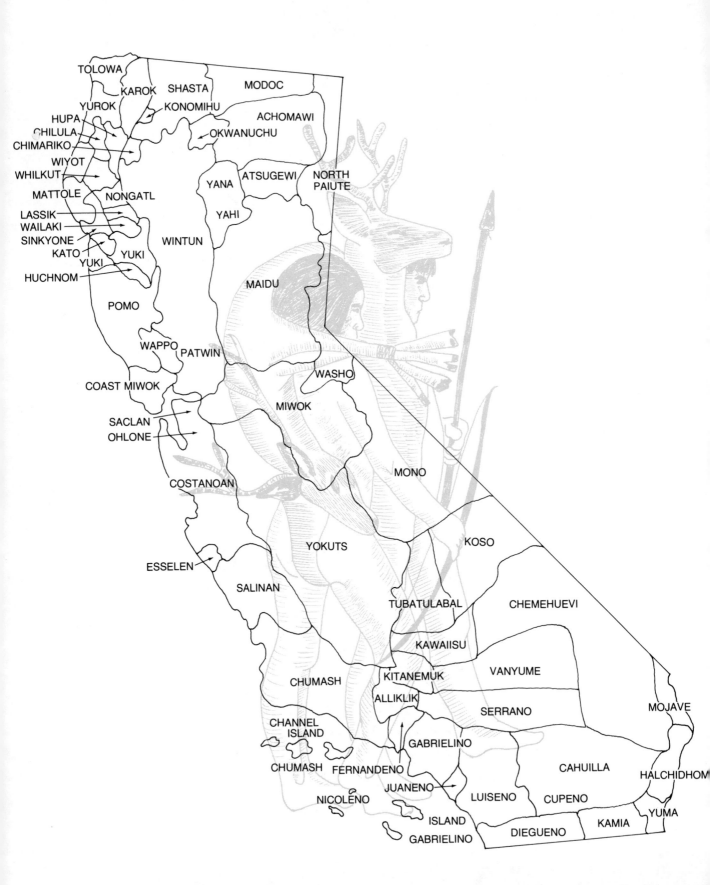

TOLOWA

KAROK SHASTA MODOC

YUROK KONOMIHU

HUPA ACHOMAWI

CHILULA OKWANUCHU

CHIMARIKO

WIYOT ATSUGEWI NORTH
PAIUTE

WHILKUT YANA

MATTOLE NONGATL

LASSIK YAHI

WAILAKI WINTUN

SINKYONE

KATO YUKI

YUKI

HUCHNOM MAIDU

POMO

WAPPO WASHO

PATWIN

COAST MIWOK MIWOK

SACLAN

OHLONE

MONO

COSTANOAN

YOKUTS KOSO

ESSELEN

SALINAN

TUBATULABAL CHEMEHUEVI

KAWAIISU

VANYUME

CHUMASH KITANEMUK

ALLIKLIK SERRANO MOJAVE

CHANNEL
ISLAND GABRIELINO

CHUMASH CAHUILLA HALCHIDHOM

FERNANDENO

JUANENO LUISENO CUPENO

NICOLENO YUMA

ISLAND KAMIA
GABRIELINO DIEGUENO

CHAPTER FOUR
NATURE'S NOURISHMENT

HUNTING AND FISHING

Indian women were responsible for the gathering of plants, seeds, nuts and berries for their families, while the men did the hunting and fishing. Indian men throughout California hunted both large and small animals. Deer, bear, elk, fox, rabbits, raccoons, squirrels and porcupines were the most common wildlife found in California. There were also quail, woodpeckers, ducks and geese. Most of the birds and animals found in California were used as food, except for the eagle, coyote, grizzly bear and skunk. Many Indians would not eat ravens, buzzards and magpies. These animals and birds were not eaten because of religious customs. The Pacific Ocean, the rivers and streams provided the Indians with a great variety of shellfish, salmon, eel and trout. They also hunted and ate insects, lizards, snakes, moles and mice.

DEER HUNTING

Deer were found all year round. The Indians used bows and arrows to kill the deer and each man learned to make his own arrow points, bows, arrowshafts and quivers. The men took very good care of their hunting tools. Often one or two men of the tribe were so skillful at making arrowheads that they made all the arrowheads for the hunters. These special craftsmen expected to share in a catch if the hunters brought back a deer.

85

The deer hunters prepared themselves **physically** as well as **spiritually** before each hunt. They lived in the **sweathouse** for several days and nights where they would sweat, **fast**, smoke and dream. If the hunter had a dream about an animal the night before the hunt, it meant that he would be successful on the hunt. Some Indian men rubbed herbs on their bodies to **disguise** their scent. Some Indians disguised themselves with animal skins and acted like deer so that they could creep close enough to their **prey** to shoot it with an arrow.

After the hunt, the deer was brought back to camp and all parts of the animal were used; the antlers were used for chipping arrowheads, the bones were used for **awls** for piercing animal skins or making baskets, the hoofs were used as rattles, the intestines were used as pouches and tying material, the skins were used for clothing and blankets, the head was cleaned and stuffed to be used as part of a hunting outfit when **stalking** deer and the meat was roasted, stewed or dried.

You know that the Indians were excellent ecologists. When they went on a game hunt, they never killed more animals than they knew their tribe could use. When they killed an animal, the Indians always said a silent prayer to the animal's spirit so that the animal would be reborn. If the Indian did not take a deer during the hunt, then the wise hunter knew that the animal was not meant to die at that time.

*   *   *   *   *

AN INDIAN LEGEND

The following story is from the Northern California Indians and is about an Indian woman who encouraged her husband to kill more owls than they really needed. She did not obey the Indian rule that the earth's gifts are not for the selfish or greedy.

*THE WOMAN WHO WAS NOT SATISFIED
"One time a man and his wife had been traveling for a great distance. Sun was going down to rest when they decided to camp in a cave until Sun woke and rose for the new day.

They were very hungry, but there was no food in the cave and that which they carried was gone.

As they made their fire, they heard the song of the horned owl a little way away from them.

The wife turned to her husband and said, 'When Owl comes near, you can shoot him and we can eat him for supper.'

The husband then got his bow and his arrows which had the tiny obsidian points used for hunting birds. When he was ready, he sang out the same way as the owl.

Owl, thinking it was one of his cousins, returned the husband's call and came closer. The husband sang out again and when Owl answered the husband knew where Owl was, and he shot one of his arrows and being a good hunter, he had meat for his supper.

Then he said to his wife, 'There is enough for now.'

'No!' said the wife, 'We have had no meat for a long time. We shall want meat for tomorrow as well, for we have far to go. And if you call them when Sun comes up, they will not come.'

*The legend, "The Woman Who Was Not Satisfied", is quoted exactly as it is printed in the Humboldt County Office of Education N.I.C.E. program.

The man heard his wife and again taking his bow and arrows, called out for more owls. The husband began shooting his arrows as fast as the owls came. But there were more owls than arrows and still they came in great numbers.

Soon they covered everything, making Night Sky, filled with bright stars, darker than before. The husband covered his wife with a blanket and fought the owls with burning sticks from Fire. But there were too many. Then they overcame the husband and wife.

And this is the way the owls paid back the greedy husband and wife for the death of their cousins."

* * * * *

The screech owl is the most common owl found in California and lives everywhere. The screech owl is not very large. It measures about eight inches in height and has a wingspread of about twenty inches. This owl has big yellow eyes, eartufts that look like horns and a bad disposition. Owls are known for their silent flight, weird shrieks and night travel. Many Indians feared owls because owls traveled at night and were associated with spirits and ghosts. Some Indians believed that an owl's call was to announce a spirit's arrival in the hereafter.

HUNTING SMALL GAME

Small game animals such as rabbits, squirrels, quail or woodpeckers were trapped and killed in several ways. Sometimes Indians shot pointed, sharpened sticks without arrowheads at rabbits and other types of small game. Rabbits were easily caught in nets, **snares** or killed with a **throwing stick**. The rabbits were skinned by the men and the women made blankets from the fur. Quail and woodpeckers were sometimes caught in basket traps. Quail have poor eyesight, but good hearing. The Indians knew that the quail usually move uphill and so traps were set on slopes. The Indians walked quietly behind the quail and the **vibrations** of the Indian's feet would drive the frightened quail uphill into the trap. Once inside the basket trap, the quail could not find a way out. The Pomo Indians used quail traps as long as 25 feet. Sometimes basket traps were tied in place over woodpecker holes in trees. When the woodpecker came out of his hole, he was trapped in the long, narrow basketry. Other Indians used **slingshots** with rocks or adobe balls to kill wild game such as ducks or geese.

Indians throughout California killed small game for food and clothing.

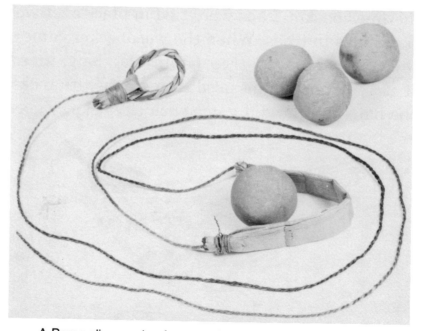

A Pomo sling made of green tule and milkweed fiber string

FISHING

Throughout California there are many lakes and rivers. Long ago, these lakes and rivers were abundantly filled with many kinds of fish. The Indians caught trout, steelhead, salmon, bass, sturgeon, perch, catfish, eel and many other varieties of fish. Fishhooks made of shell or bone were mainly used when the Indians fished along the ocean shore or when fishing on lakes. Nets, spears, basket traps and **weirs** were used in streams and rivers. A weir is like a **latticework** dam made of **vertical** poles and cross pieces of branches. The poles were set like **tripods** to make the weir sturdy and then small branches were woven in and out of the poles to keep the fish from getting through, except for one narrow opening. As the fish swam through this narrow opening, the Indians were able to catch the fish by hand, by spearing them or by using dip nets. The Hupa were one of the tribes to use a weir or fish dam.

Basket traps for catching fish were large, coarsely woven baskets made so that the fish could swim in one end and not find their way out. Eels were also caught in this manner.

Spears were used by every Indian in California who fished in large bodies of water. The long, slender spear shaft was good for jabbing. Some spear shafts, like arrowshafts, had a main shaft and a foreshaft. The foreshaft was usually double pronged, one **prong** being slightly longer than the other. Each prong had sharp **barbs** or points made of bone or flint and these barbs were glued to each foreshaft with pitch or asphaltum, then tightly wrapped with milkweed or iris fiber. The end of the fiber that held the barbs in place was then fastened to the main shaft of the spear. When the fish was speared, the foreshaft of the spear would detach, but the fiber that connected the foreshaft to the main shaft would allow the fisherman to pull the fish and foreshaft to shore.

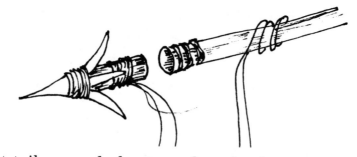

Most tribes used plants such as buckeye or soaproot to **paralyze** the fish. These plants were pounded and scattered over the top of the water. The crushed plants would paralyze the fish and the fish would float to the surface of the water where the Indians would net them or scoop them out barehanded and throw them ashore. While the men fished, women cleaned and prepared the catch. They cut the fish into strips and dried them. They caught only as much fish as their families could use.

The Pomo Indians of the Clear Lake area often caught fish called hitch. The Indians cooked these fish for many hours in underground ovens. This long, slow cooking process softened the bones of the hitch so that the Indians could eat the entire fish, bones and all! Any extra amounts of fish were dried. Some of the dried fish, including the bones, was ground into a coarse powder. This fish meal could be stored for later use.

Hupa salmon dam

EEL AND SALMON

The Indians of Northern California had eel and salmon ceremonies. When the eels and salmon traveled up the rivers from the ocean, the people held special ceremonies to celebrate the arrival of the salmon and eels. The eels lived in the rivers all year long, but in the late summer, the eels started down toward the sea to lay eggs in the part of the ocean where they had been hatched. Indians caught the eels with nets and traps. The salmon, however, lived in the ocean and swam up the rivers to lay eggs in the rivers where they were born. The Hupa Indians had a First Salmon Ceremony in the spring and throughout the summer, the people caught salmon in large nets. In September or October, the Hupa Indians built a fish dam in the Trinity River for the fall salmon run. The salmon and eels were roasted and eaten during these special ceremonies. The eel and salmon meat, as well as salmon eggs, were smoked and dried for winter storage.

* * * * *

AN INDIAN LEGEND

The eel is a long snakelike fish without bones. In the following legend, the eel meets the sucker fish and you will find out how the eel loses its bones. This legend is told by the Hupa, Karok and Yurok Indians.

*THE SUCKER AND THE EEL

"A long time ago, Eel and Sucker played a card game with sticks.

Sucker was very, very lucky that day and Eel was very unlucky.

The two of them played their game until night and when they stopped, the Sucker had won all of the Eel's fine furs, all of his shell money, all of his best baskets, and even had won his house.

The Eel was worried and sad. He sat thinking for a long time.

At last he said, 'Sucker, I'm going to play you one more game and I'll bet my bones I'll win this one.'

They played again and again the Sucker won. That is why today Sucker has so many bones and Eel has none."

* * * * *

*The legend, "The Sucker and the Eel", is quoted exactly as it is printed in the Humboldt County Office of Education N.I.C.E. program.

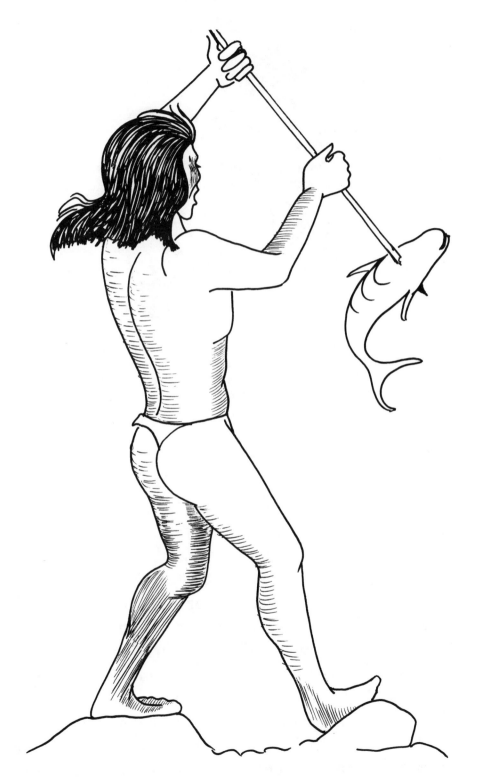

The Indians speared fish in the rivers, lakes and streams of California.

Indians in the Carquinez Strait baited animal flesh on a long, strong rope made of thick fibers. When a sturgeon or other large fish swallowed the bait, a barb would stick in the throat of the fish. Several Indians were sometimes needed to drag the fish from the water when it tired out. A sturgeon would sometimes be four to six feet long!

FOODS FROM THE SEA

The Indians who lived near the sea coast ate many varieties of seafood such as oysters, mussels, clams, barnacles, chitons, sea urchins, snails, crabs, abalone, octopus, sea bass, salmon and sturgeon. These seafoods were usually roasted over fires or steamed in underground ovens. They were also dried and smoked for future use. As the Indians prepared and ate shellfish, they threw the shells in the same place until a mound or hill was formed from these shells. Sometimes other things such as tools, weapons, animal and bird bones have been found in these shell mounds or **middens**. Many ancient village sites have been uncovered in the San Francisco Bay Area. There is a two thousand year old shell mound near Fremont that can be visited. Other Indian shell mounds are located in San Mateo, the San Joaquin Delta, the Santa Barbara Channel, Humboldt Bay, San Diego and in many other areas along the California coast. Today, most of these shell mounds have disappeared under the foundations of restaurants, beach-front homes and land fill.

Some Indians used sea otters, seals and sea lions for food and skins. Men swam to offshore rocks to kill these animals. Some Indians reached the rocks by using canoes or rafts. These men imitated the actions of the sea lions as they crept close enough to club the animal to death. The dead animals were towed back to shore by swimmers or canoes. On land, the animals were skinned and prepared for cooking. Other times, the dead sea lions were skinned and cleaned on the rocks where they were killed. The meat was then packed into canoes and taken to shore. The tusks of the sea lion were highly prized and used as necklaces or as ornaments on ceremonial costumes.

This Hupa headband is made from the tusks of sea lions.

WHALES

Whales were frequently seen during certain periods going north and south from Alaska to Baja California. These **mammals** traveled in herds and were respected and known to the Indians as spirits of the sea as well as another source of food. The California Indians usually did not **venture** out to hunt these animals, but we know that whales were used because whale **vertebrae** have been found in some of the coastal shell mounds. Indians used whale meat from a whale that had washed ashore because the mammal had grown weak or helpless and could not continue its journey. The knowledge that one of these huge mammals had been beached brought many days of feasting to the Indians. The meat was roasted and eaten and extra meat was cut in strips and dried for winter storage.

Whale meat was highly prized by the Indians. The meat is rich in oil and high in vitamins. Dried whale meat was often traded.

SEA BIRDS

Sea birds were also eaten by the Indians who lived along the coast. Some of these sea birds included sea gulls, cormorants, cranes, herons, pelicans, terns and others. Most sea birds lay their eggs in carefully built nests, but a few lay their eggs on ledges of rocks. Eggs supplied the Indians' diet with protein. Eggs were considered a **delicacy** and at certain times of the year, Indians along the coast boated to offshore islands to collect these eggs.

Snowy egrets were found among the marshlands and tules throughout California. The hollow leg bones of the heron and egret were used as whistles and flutes in dance ceremonies.

INTERESTING THOUGHTS

The Indians spent most of the year hunting, gathering, drying, preparing and storing nuts, roots, seeds, meat and fish for the long, cold months when their world would be caught in winter's grip. As the days grew shorter and the nights grew colder, the families gathered together in their warm winter shelters. They wrapped themselves **snuggly** in the soft warmth of their skin blankets and held out their hands and spirits to the heat of the fire. Occasionally, a person would rise to poke the fire and add more wood. The new firewood sparked and snapped and sent orange and black cinders drifting through the smoke hole in the roof of the shelter. The brightness from the newly **stoked** fire shone on the contented faces of the small children as they nestled closer to their parents. Now was the time when the elders of the tribe told the creation stories. Everyone sat and listened to the elders tell the stories that had been told to them when they were young. The children sat wide-eyed listening to the legends explain how and why their people came to be. And so, the storms of winter passed until it was time once again to begin anew the gathering and collecting of nature's nourishment.

BACKTRACKING

Can you answer the following questions?
(1) Name some animals Indians hunted for food.
(2) What animals did the Indians **not** kill for food? Why?
(3) Tell two ways the deer hunters prepared themselves before a hunt.
(4) What lesson or moral does the legend "The Woman Who Was Not Satisfied" teach you?
(5) Name three ways Indians killed small game.
(6) What is a weir? How was it used by the Indians? Name two other ways Indians caught fish.
(7) What is the advantage of an arrow with a foreshaft?
(8) What types of seafood were eaten by the Indians living along the coast?
(9) What is a shell mound? Why are shell mounds of importance to us today?
(10) Briefly describe a winter evening in an Indian shelter.

*For Wise Eagles: Indians had several ways of killing fish and game. Are some of these ways still in use today? Tell about them.

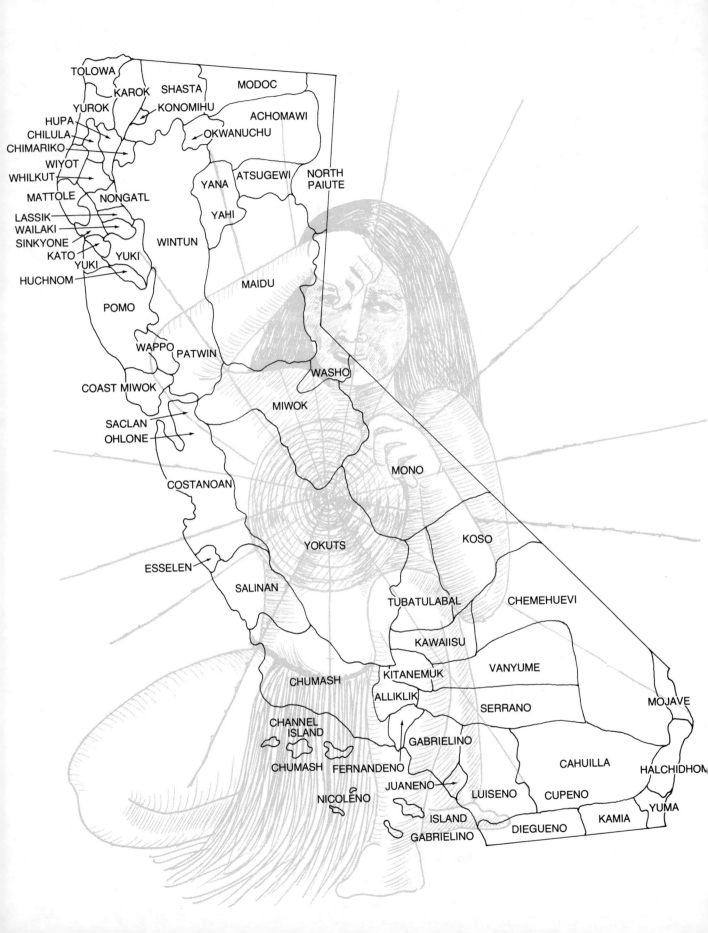

TOLOWA

KAROK

SHASTA

MODOC

KONOMIHU

ACHOMAWI

YUROK

HUPA

OKWANUCHU

CHILULA

CHIMARIKO

WIYOT

YANA

ATSUGEWI

NORTH
PAIUTE

WHILKUT

YAHI

MATTOLE

NONGATL

LASSIK

WAILAKI

WINTUN

SINKYONE

KATO

YUKI

YUKI

HUCHNOM

MAIDU

POMO

WAPPO

PATWIN

WASHO

COAST MIWOK

MIWOK

SACLAN

OHLONE

MONO

COSTANOAN

YOKUTS

KOSO

ESSELEN

SALINAN

TUBATULABAL

CHEMEHUEVI

KAWAIISU

VANYUME

KITANEMUK

CHUMASH

ALLIKLIK

SERRANO

MOJAVE

CHANNEL
ISLAND

GABRIELINO

CHUMASH

FERNANDENO

CAHUILLA

HALCHIDHOM

JUANENO

NICOLENO

LUISENO

CUPENO

YUMA

ISLAND

DIEGUENO

KAMIA

GABRIELINO

CHAPTER FIVE

USING NATURE'S GIFTS FOR BASKETS, BOWLS AND BOATS

BASKET MAKING

Indians in all of North America made baskets, but the baskets made in California were especially fine. The valleys of Northern and Southern California were filled with many kinds of coarse, tough, tall grasses and other natural materials.

Some of nature's gifts that the Northern Indians used to weave fine, beautiful baskets were **supple** twigs from willow and redbud trees and roots from sedge and bulrush. Some coarse baskets were made entirely of willow or tule. The root of sedge was one of the more important materials the Northern California Indians used for weaving baskets. Sedge roots were cleaned and stripped and put into rolls like twine. Sometimes this material was put into wet ashes to turn it permanently black. The Indians used black in many of their basket designs. This color never faded. Another color commonly used was red. Bark from the redbud tree was gathered and used for red designs in many baskets. Grasses could also be dyed by soaking them in dark colored mud or in the juice of manzanita berries, wild mustard or onion skin. Shells as well as feathers from ducks, meadowlarks, wild canaries, woodpeckers and other native birds added more color and beauty to the exceptional baskets of the California Indians.

The Cahuilla, Luiseno, Diegueno and other Indian tribes of Southern California used several materials for basket making. These materials included a grass called Epicampes rigens, used for the base or foundation of the baskets, and juncus and sumac reeds used for weaving the basket coils together. The grass (Epicampes rigens) was collected, dried, tied into bundles and stored in the homes of the Indians so it was handy for basket making. The weaving materials, juncus and sumac, added color to the baskets. The sumac gave a light straw color. It was sometimes dyed a very deep black by soaking for a week or longer in elderberry juice. The juncus reed was known for three basic colors: red, brown and yellow. This was a popular reed for basket making.

There were two main types of woven baskets: twined and coiled. Twined basketry is found among Indian people to the north of Lake County, such as the Shasta, Hupa, Yurok, Tolowa, Modoc and Northern Wintun tribes. Coiled basketry is common among Indians to the south, such as the Gabrielino, Luiseno, Cahuilla and Serrano tribes. The Pomo Indians sometimes combined the two types of basketry.

Some twined baskets were made for rough use, such as for holding acorns when they were pounded, backpack baskets and for packing freshly gathered acorns. Some of these baskets were woven tightly enough to hold water or mush.

Coiled baskets were used for cooking. So tightly were these baskets woven that they could hold water without leaking. Red hot stones were picked up with looped sticks. The Indians lowered these hot stones into a basket full of acorn mush and gradually the mixture in the basket began to boil. The Indian women constantly stirred this mixture so the hot rocks would not burn the bottom of the basket. As the mush began to boil, the rocks were removed, washed and returned to the fire pit to be reheated and used again and again.

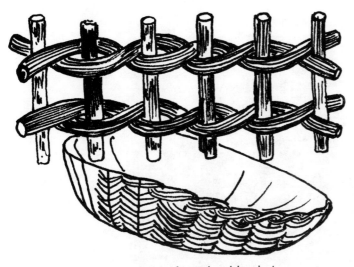

The beginnings of a twined basket

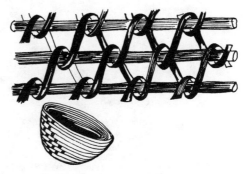

The beginnings of a coiled basket

Chumash Indian women living on the Santa
Barbara coast and Channel Islands also wove baskets.
They poured melted asphaltum on the inside of some
baskets. When the asphaltum was cool, the baskets
were waterproof and could be used for cooking. Indian
women of the southern deserts and mountain areas
used **pitch** to line baskets.

A woman might work for a year or more creating a
single basket depending upon her design and whether
or not her basket materials were available. Personal
pride went into the construction and design of each
basket.

An unfinished basket made by a Karok Indian in the year 1903

Among the Pomo Indians and a few nearby tribes, both men and women made baskets. The men made open work baskets, such as fish traps, baby carriers and rough twined baskets. The Pomo women made tightly woven baskets with **intricate** designs. The Pomo women used a greater variety of designs in their baskets than most other tribes. A woman's basket design was so **unique** that she could always identify her basket among others by looking carefully at the design. Pomo women never completed a design. There was always a break or **dau** in the design to keep away evil spirits. Dating from earliest times, the Pomos were the first people in California to decorate their baskets with feathers. Other tribes used feathers, but in earliest times, never covered the entire basket with feathers as the Pomos did. The Pomo basketry is still considered among the finest examples of basket art, because of their creativity in decorating their baskets with shells, feathers and combinations of designs.

From old to new—An eighty year old leaching basket—A two hundred year old grinding stone and baskets recently made by the Pomo Indians

Pomo miniature coiled baskets

This Mesa Grande basket is from Southern California and can be seen in the San Diego Museum of Man. It was made in 1936. As the grasses have aged, they have changed color from white to brown.

These Indian baskets can be seen in the Oakland Museum.

The Achomawi or Pit River Indians made this twined basket.

In 1907, the small basket was purchased from an Ohlone Indian in Santa Clara. It is believed that the basket was made by Tulare Indians.

This large bowl-like basket is said to have been in a family since 1796! It was purchased by C. Hart Merriam in 1907.

Circular winnower or sifter purchased by C. Hart Merriam from the only survivor of the Oomontwash tribe (Ohlone), September, 1902

An old seed beater

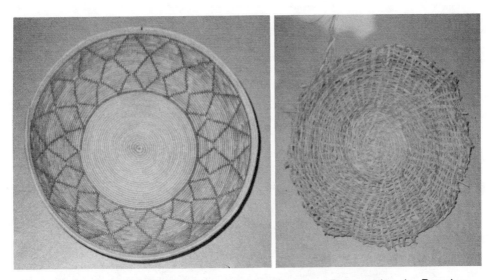

Baskets from the Malki Museum on the Morongo Reservation in Banning, California

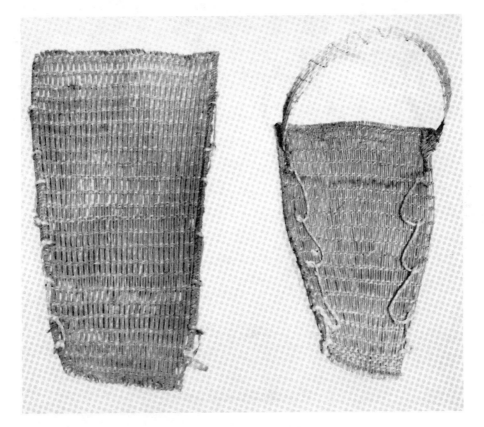

Cradles for infants were woven by the Yokuts Indians. Newborn babies were strapped in these cradles.

Dat sa Lee, a Paiute Indian, made this beautiful basket called "The Fledglings".

BOWLS

Some of the Indians who lived in Southern California used clay for making cooking utensils, such as bowls, cups and jars. They learned this art from the Yuma and Colorado River tribes. Some of the Indians put finely crushed rock into the clay to make it firmer and stronger. The pottery maker always used a wooden paddle and a smoothing stone. The pottery was built in coils much like the baskets. After drying, the pots were baked in a fire. The art of using clay for pottery is a native discovery and dates back to the earliest times.

Chumash Indians in Southern California used a soft, smooth stone called **soapstone** to make bowls. Soapstone bowls made better cooking bowls than baskets or clay pots. People of other tribes were always glad to trade for them. Some of these soapstone bowls have been found in California's Great Central Valley and north of the San Francisco Bay Area. This shows that many tribes of Indians traded with one another.

Coastal Indians used abalone shells for bowls and eating utensils. The Channel Island Chumash Indians of Southern California made food bowls by plugging the **siphon** holes of abalone shells with asphaltum. Sometimes the asphaltum in the holes of the shells was also decorated with tiny inlaid discs of abalone shell. The handwork put into the decorations on these bowls is seldom found on items used today.

The Indians near the Colorado River made jars of twisted grass. The jars were heavily plastered with mud and allowed to dry. These jars were used for storing seeds, nuts and grains. The sticks in the background are digging sticks used for digging bulbs and roots.

These ancient clay jars were discovered in Southern California caves. These jars were used as storage for seeds, grain and water. The Indians would leave these filled jars in caves for use in times of need. At times, they placed a spirit stick with the clay jars to protect the jars and their contents from trespassers.

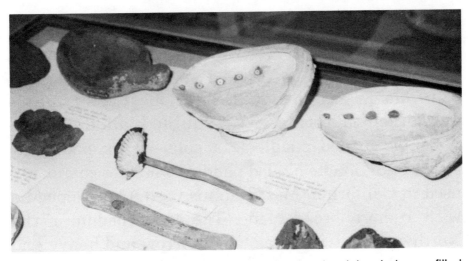

These abalone shells were used as bowls. Notice that the siphon holes are filled with asphaltum and decorated with clam shell discs.

TULE BOATS

The Indians also used nature's gifts to build boats. There were three main types of boats used by the native Californians. These were (1) the tule boat, (2) the dug-out canoe and (3) the plank boat.

The Indians who lived in areas where tules grew often made tule boats. These boats were made by tying large bundles of tules together with strong vines. A man could kneel or stand in the tule boat and **pole** himself across calm waters. The tule boat was high in the front and back and lower on the sides. The boatman who kneeled or sat in these tule crafts did not have the comfort of a sturdier boat. If the tule boat was not woven tightly enough, then the boatman would find himself kneeling in several inches of water. Tule boats did not last long and were usually good for less than a year. Tule boats had to be pulled out of the water after they were used so they would not get **soggy** and sink.

In San Francisco Bay, the Ohlone Indians **navigated** their tule boats with a **double bladed paddle.** A double bladed paddle is a pole with a paddle at either end. Double bladed paddles were not commonly used in California. Most Indians used a single paddle with a short, broad blade. The canoe paddle of the Northwestern tribes was long, narrow and heavy and was used as a pole and an oar. The double bladed paddle was used mainly by the San Francisco Bay Area Indians and the Channel Island Indians in the South.

Tules were used for boats because they are light and buoyant. Look carefully at the double bladed paddle used by the Bay Area and Channel Island Indians. Do you think the double bladed paddle was better than a single bladed paddle? Why? Do you think it was easier to navigate a tule boat with a double bladed paddle?

DUG-OUT CANOE

A **dug-out** canoe was another type of boat made by the native Californians. The dug-out canoes of the Yuroks were made from cedar logs or redwood logs. The logs were hollowed out by burning and then the soft **scorched** wood was scraped out with an **adze.** The Indian craftsmen worked slowly and carefully because a slight mistake could change the whole shape of the boat. It was important to keep the sides and bottom a certain thickness. By tapping and listening to the sides of the canoe, the craftsmen could tell when the proper thickness of the boat was reached. It might take a year or two to make one of these boats.

Most craftsmen made their boats **watertight** by using pitch or asphaltum to seal out moisture. The Yurok craftsmen of the North would spread wooden shavings inside the canoe. These shavings were burned and pitch that oozed from the shavings made the boat watertight. The Yuroks had to be very careful because if the fire got too hot, the boat might crack. The Yurok boats were highly prized as trade items by other Indian tribes. The Yurok canoes were used on rivers such as the Shasta River, Klamath River, Eel River, Salmon River, Trinity River and Pit River. These canoes were also sturdy enough to be used on the ocean waters along the coast.

Dug-out canoes made from pine, cedar or fir logs were found in other parts of California and used on rivers, creeks, lakes and marshes. They were burned and dug out, but the finished boat did not have as much detailed workmanship as the canoes of the North.

Dug-out canoes were of different lengths. Some were as long as twenty feet.
You can see the carved seats in this canoe used by the Hupa Indians in 1902.

The Channel Island Indians used plank boats. The captains or owners of the

PLANK BOATS

Plank boats were made by the Chumash and the Gabrielino Indians of Southern California. In the mountains above their seashore homes these Indians split pine logs into planks by using bone wedges. These planks were carried to the seashore villages where the planks were shaped. The planks were then skillfully fastened together with fiber cords that were passed through small holes in the planks. When the canoe was finished, the Indians melted asphaltum and poured it along the edges where the planks came together and into the holes where the cords or thongs were tied. These boats were used in the waters of the Channel Islands. They could hold as many as twenty people and were navigated by men kneeling on the bottom of the boats using double bladed paddles. The Indians were excellent boatmen. They made frequent trips from the villages on the coast to those on the Channel Islands.

The Indians of California respected and cared for their boats. These wooden boats were used for many years and often were passed on from generation to generation.

agoing vessels were highly respected by other members of their tribes.

INTERESTING THOUGHTS

Nature filled the valleys, creeks and rivers of California with reeds, grasses and trees. With these gifts, the Indians created beautiful baskets. Making a basket involved a great deal of time, patience and creativity. Indian women waited for the right season to find and gather the needed plant materials. Then they dried and stored these materials until they were ready to create a basket.

Today, some Indian women carry on the traditions of the past by making beautiful baskets. These skilled **artisans** find that the materials once available for basket making are no longer easily found. The land has been fenced off and built upon and many areas where basket materials could be gathered are now gone. Today's basket makers continue to search for roots, twigs, grasses and reeds in many locations. At Indian fairs, women who make baskets gather together and exchange information on new sources of plant materials. Sometimes materials can be purchased at these fairs, but the old traditions of making the baskets still remain.

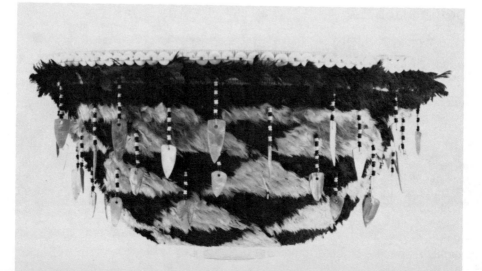

BACKTRACKING

Can you answer the following questions?
(1)   Name five (5) materials the Indians used in their basketry.
(2)   How did the Indians add colors to their baskets? What two colors were the most common? How did they get these colors?
(3)   What were the two (2) main types of baskets? What were the different uses for these baskets?
(4)   How was acorn mush cooked in baskets?
(5)   What other materials were used for making cooking utensils?
(6)a. Name the three main types of boats used by the California Indians.
   b. Name the general areas where each type of boat was made.
(7)   What are the advantages and disadvantages of a tule boat?
(8)   Name three ways asphaltum was used in the making of bowls, baskets and boats.

*For Wise Eagles: What is the difference between a single and double bladed paddle? How do you think each would effect the speed and steering of a boat?

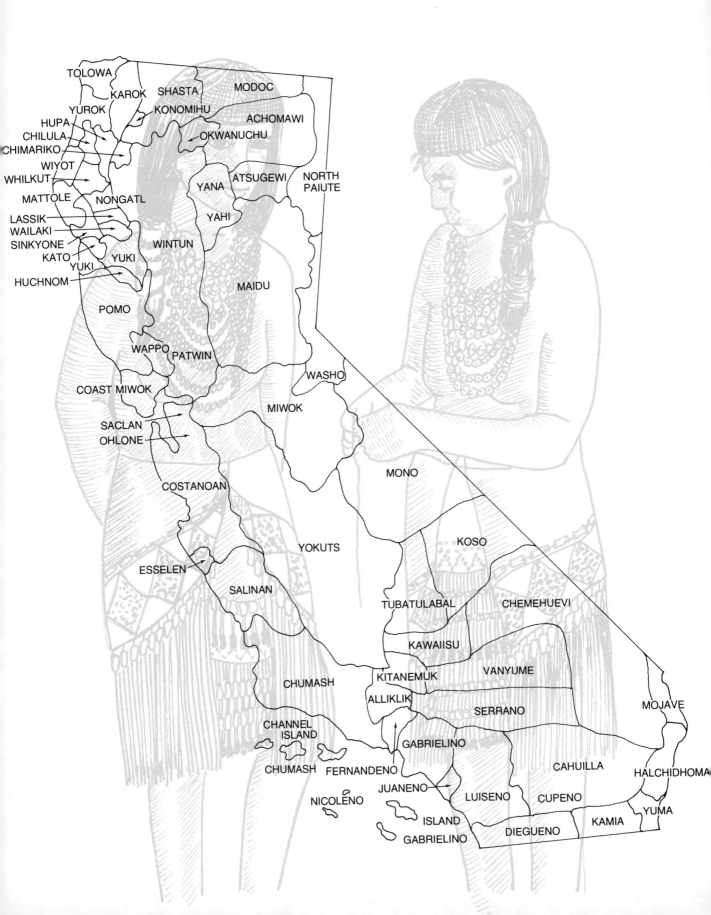

TOLOWA
KAROK
SHASTA
MODOC
YUROK
KONOMIHU
ACHOMAWI
HUPA
OKWANUCHU
CHILULA
CHIMARIKO
WIYOT
YANA
ATSUGEWI
NORTH
PAIUTE
WHILKUT
MATTOLE
NONGATL
YAHI
LASSIK
WAILAKI
WINTUN
SINKYONE
KATO
YUKI
YUKI
HUCHNOM
POMO
MAIDU
WAPPO
PATWIN
WASHO
COAST MIWOK
MIWOK
SACLAN
OHLONE
MONO
COSTANOAN
YOKUTS
KOSO
ESSELEN
SALINAN
TUBATULABAL
CHEMEHUEVI
KAWAIISU
VANYUME
KITANEMUK
CHUMASH
ALLIKLIK
SERRANO
MOJAVE
CHANNEL
ISLAND
GABRIELINO
CHUMASH
CAHUILLA
HALCHIDHOMA
FERNANDENO
JUANENO
NICOLEÑO
LUISENO
CUPENO
YUMA
ISLAND
GABRIELINO
DIEGUENO
KAMIA

CHAPTER SIX
CLOTHING OF THE INDIANS

EVERYDAY WEAR

Throughout most of the year, California weather is warm and sunny. Because of this pleasant climate, the Indians wore very little clothing. Clothing that was worn by the Indians was made from animal skins and plant fibers.

During the warmer months of the year, the men wore nothing at all or a **loincloth** of buckskin. A loincloth is a piece of deerskin hung, front and back, from a beltlike strip of leather called a **thong**. The thong circled the man's waist. The thong was an important piece of clothing for a man because, like a belt, he could use it as a holder for a flint or obsidian knife, a rabbit stick or a skin pouch. An Indian woman's clothing was a two-piece skirt made of a small front apron and a larger back apron. The skirt was made of shredded plant **fibers** or animal skins. Materials commonly used were strips of tule, willow bark, cedar bark, agave fiber, bear grass, milkweed fiber or Indian hemp. This type of skirt was worn by all the Indian women of California and became known as the "California Apron". Children under ten years old wore no clothing, but children over ten years followed the clothing habits of their fathers or mothers.

COLDER DAYS

When the cold weather forced the Indians to wear more protection, men, women and children wore a skin blanket wrapped around their shoulders. The blankets used for warmth during the day were often used as bed coverings at night.

Throughout California, the most popular type of blanket was made with rabbit skins. The entire rabbit hide was cut into one circular piece with an obsidian blade knife. A skillful Indian could cut one hide into a ribbon twelve or fifteen feet long. Several rabbit skins were cut in this manner and tied together to form a chain forty or more feet long. This long fur chain was tied to a tree and twisted into a fur rope and allowed to dry into curled forms. After several of these fur chains had been twisted and allowed to dry, they were woven together with milkweed fibers or hemp into a very warm covering. An adult's blanket required a hundred skins while a child's blanket took about fifty skins. Other highly prized skins for blankets were made from sea otters, deer and wildcats.

Rabbit skins were twisted into fur ropes and sewn together with plant fiber. Rabbit skin blankets were important to many California Indians. They were used throughout the year during the cool parts of the days or evenings.

Every member of an Indian family had his own skin blanket. In the colder parts of California, these blankets could mean the difference between life and death. From infants to the elders, skin blankets were an important part of the Indians' everyday life.

Hupa man

TANNING HIDES

When the Indians used deerskins for blankets or clothing, they usually **tanned** the hides. The hide was soaked in water and buried in wet ground for several days to loosen the hair on the hide. Then the Indian used a scraper made of a deer rib to remove the hair from the hide. The Indian had to be a skilled craftsman to remove the hair without cutting through the hide. After the hair was removed, the hide was put into a special tanning preparation of deer brains and oak gall and soaked. The hides were stretched, pulled and kneaded until they were soft and could be made into blankets, loincloths, skirts, capes, **moccasins** and dance costumes. The softest deerskins were used as baby blankets.

FOOTWEAR

Most of the California Indians did not wear foot coverings except during the cold winter months or on long journeys. One type of foot covering was ankle-high skin moccasins. These moccasins were made from a single piece of buckskin and seamed up the heel and front with plant fiber. This type of low, single-piece moccasin was worn by Indians such as the Miwoks, Wintuns, Hupa and Yuroks. During cold weather, the moccasins were sometimes lined with grass for added warmth. The Modoc, Shasta, Northern Paiute and Maidu Indians wore heavier moccasins because of the colder climate and rougher **terrain**.

The Lassik tribe, an Indian group close to the Hupa Indians, did not make their moccasins like those of their neighbors. The Lassiks made their moccasins with a single seam going from the little toe to the outer ankle.

Some of the Central and Northwestern tribes used strips of deerskin as drawstrings to hold the moccasins on their feet. Each tribe had different ways of tying the drawstrings. Some tribes tied them around the front, back or side of the ankle. Other tribes wrapped the drawstrings around the **instep** of the foot and brought them around to be tied behind the heel.

The Indians seamed their moccasins in different ways. Have you noticed that some shoes manufactured today are patterned like Indian moccasins for comfort and ease of wearing?

Most of the Indians of Southern California went barefoot because of the warm climate, but on long journeys they would sometimes wear sandals made of yucca fiber or Indian hemp. The desert Indians, however, when traveling in the mountainous area surrounding their desert home, wore skin moccasins that reached high up the calf of the leg.

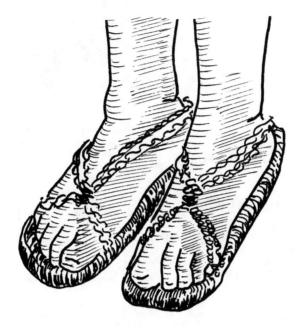

Sandals were made of plant fiber and worn by some of the Indians of the Great Central Valley and Southern California.

Indians living along the coast or near mud flats and marshes used tules to make large round frames for their feet. The Indians could walk in muddy areas without sinking when wearing these frames on their feet.

In the winter, some Indians wrapped their feet in fur such as rabbit skin. This type of fur boot covered the feet and ankles and was tied around the ankle with a thong. Sometimes these fur coverings were attached to a wooden frame that had been laced with wild grapevine. These wooden frames were clever devices for moving about in the snow. Modern day snowshoes are probably fashioned after the frames that the Indians made.

Making a frame for the feet

THREAD AND CORD

The women made their own thread and cord for sewing. This thread and cord was made from iris leaves, nettles, agave, milkweed or Indian hemp plants. The plants were pounded until all that was left was strong, stringlike fibers. A woman would take a fiber and roll it up and down her bare thigh and as she added more fibers the cord would grow longer and thicker. When she rolled two pieces of cord together, it made a strong, tightly twisted double cord. Sometimes the cord was light and fine and sometimes it was thick and heavy, but it was always strong. Cord was used for many things such as sewing clothing and moccasins, making rabbit nets, fishnets and carrying nets. Some Indian men of Southern California helped make the thread and cord for their families.

BASKET CAPS

Throughout California many Indian women wore woven basket caps. These caps were worn by some women every day as part of their dress. These caps were beautifully woven and were not only decorative to the women, but were useful as well. In some tribes, when a woman went out to gather firewood, plants, roots or seeds, she wore a tump line over her basket cap to help support a large burden basket on her back. When the burden basket was filled, it was held firmly in place by the tump line that went over the woman's basket cap. In some tribes, such as the Northern Maidu, men, women and children wore basket caps.

The basket cap helped to protect the Indian woman's forehead from the rubbing of a tump line.

CEREMONIAL COSTUMES

Most of the California Indians had special costumes to wear for **ceremonial** occasions, such as marking the seasons, coming of age of boys and girls, re-enacting tales from the family history, funerals, creation pageants, acorn gathering and deer hunting. They used many types of decorations on their costumes such as eagle feathers, shells, walrus tusks, bones, claws and **juniper** berries to make their dance costumes handsome.

Headbands were made and worn to ceremonial feasts and dances. These headbands were made from the feathers of the red shafted flicker, the red-headed woodpecker, hawks, eagles, the yellow hammer, and sometimes the magpie and other birds. Some headbands were made from mole fur and decorated with clam shell discs.

In certain ceremonies, Indians such as the Pomo and Hupa wore feather headbands across their foreheads just above their eyes. The feathers in the headbands were cut with obsidian knives to resemble miniature arrows. These feathers were glued to the headbands with the sticky juice from milkweed plants or glue made from sturgeon. The ends of the headbands flipped back and forth as the dancers moved. Occasionally, Indians combined the headbands with small headdresses made of magpie feathers. The headdresses were bound to their heads with leather thongs. The Pomo Indians sometimes wore cap-like woven wigs. Feathers were glued to the ends of sticks that were stuck into these wigs. These headdresses were very **elaborate** and a sight to behold.

Some ceremonial costumes were made with straps of eagle down or hawk feathers that crisscrossed over the wearer's chest and tied around the waist. A skin or feather skirt was worn. Some Indians, such as the Northern Miwoks, nearly always wore a cape of eagle, hawk or other feathers. To add to these costumes, Indians wore strings of clam shell disc beads.

Men usually made the dance costumes for both men and women. No two costumes were the same—they were quite colorful and decorated with clam shell discs and feathers in many designs. These costumes took many hours to make and were highly prized as heirlooms. Some of these magnificent costumes can be seen today in local museums.

This Wintun Indian is wearing a feather cape and dancing in front of an earth-covered dance house in Cortina Valley, Colusa County. The picture was taken in the year 1906.

TATTOOING

Many Indians of California had their faces or bodies tattooed. Among the tribes, tattooing was applied to a person at any age. Many Indians could apply the tattooing, but some were considered better at tattooing than others. Some Indians of Southern California tattooed the upper part of their bodies while other Southern California Indians only tattooed their foreheads or chins. Some women covered their bodies from the waist to the chin with tattoo marks that were very decorative. This tattooing was so **intricate** that from a distance one might think that the woman was wearing a **garment**! Along the Colorado River, the Southern tribes wore tattoos on their foreheads and the women tattooed lines on their chins. Some Indian women of the Wintun, Yuki and Pomo tribes tattooed marks on their chins as a sign of womanhood. Some tattoo lines told how old a woman was or to what family group she belonged. Also, among some Indian tribes, tattoo marks were believed to show the way into the spirit world after death. Some Indians believed that certain tattoo marks would give them safe passage to another world.

Tattoo marks were made by pricking a pattern or design on the skin with a very sharp thorn, sharpened bone or sliver of stone. When the blood oozed out of the pricked areas, colors were rubbed into the wounds. This was a very painful **procedure**. If an Indian had been tattooed on the face, he ate only very soft foods for a few days so as not to crack open the scabs. He or she also slept face up so that the tattoo would heal straight.

Green coloring for tattooing was made from the juice of the green leaves of the soap plant. Black coloring could also be made from the soap plant by baking the root and mixing the juice with charcoal. Poison oak juice or sap mixed with charcoal ashes was another source of black coloring. The Indians had many sources of color for tattooing, but once an Indian was tattooed, the marks could not be removed.

Face and chin tattooing

BODY AND FACE PAINTING

Many Indians of California painted their bodies and faces. The Diegueno Indians of the South painted their faces for ceremonies and sometimes for every day. The men and women used many different designs.

The Mojave Indians painted their faces every day. The Mojave Indians painted their faces not only for decoration, but also to protect their skin against the weather and insects. A Mojave Indian painted his face with a design that he especially liked and when he got tired of it, he would select another common pattern. Only rarely did a Mojave Indian create an entirely new pattern. Mojave women could not use black face painting, but could apply small amounts of black below their eyes to lessen the glare of the desert sun. White paint was used on the body, but usually not on the face. The Mojave Indians had a custom of saving red or black paint to be sprinkled over their bodies when they died.

The Chumash of the Santa Barbara area used stripes of white paint on their faces and bodies. This white paint was made from a certain kind of **plumbiferous** stone. Body painting was used when celebrating and dancing.

The Yokuts also painted their faces and bodies with paint made from red and white earth and black charcoal or **graphite.** Before the paint was applied to the body, it was mixed with bear or elk grease so that it made a smooth, thick paste. The Yokuts did not use paint on their faces and bodies every day, but painting was used for special dances or ceremonies.

Some tribes also made black paint for body and face painting by mixing charcoal with the juice of a baked soap root. White paint was sometimes made from powdered steatite (soapstone) and red paint was made from ground cinnabar. Body paints could be washed away by bathing in a stream or river.

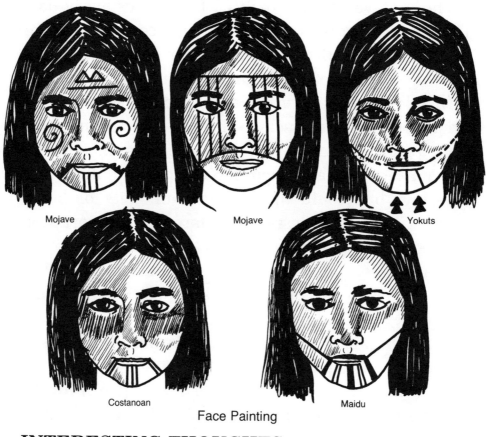

Mojave   Mojave   Yokuts

Costanoan   Maidu

Face Painting

INTERESTING THOUGHTS

Throughout California the Indians' everyday clothing was similar. The women wore the skirt known as the "California Apron" and the men went without clothing or wore a loincloth. The Indians used nature's gifts for everyday clothing and they also developed **distinctive** and beautiful ceremonial costumes.

BACKTRACKING

Can you answer the following questions?
(1) Indian women wore double aprons made of plant fiber or skins. What would be the advantages of wearing a double apron?
(2) How did the Indians make string or cord? What were some uses for this string or cord?
(3) What did the Indians use to decorate their costumes?
(4) Why do you think some of the Indians had their faces or bodies tattooed?
(5) Why do you think some of the Indians used body or face paint?
(6) Why did some Indian women wear basket caps?

*For Wise Eagles: Can you think of people today who use body paint as well as elaborate costumes in their work?

*For Wise Eagles: Some Indians of the desert used black paint under their eyes to lessen glare. Can you think of any people today who might use this Indian idea?

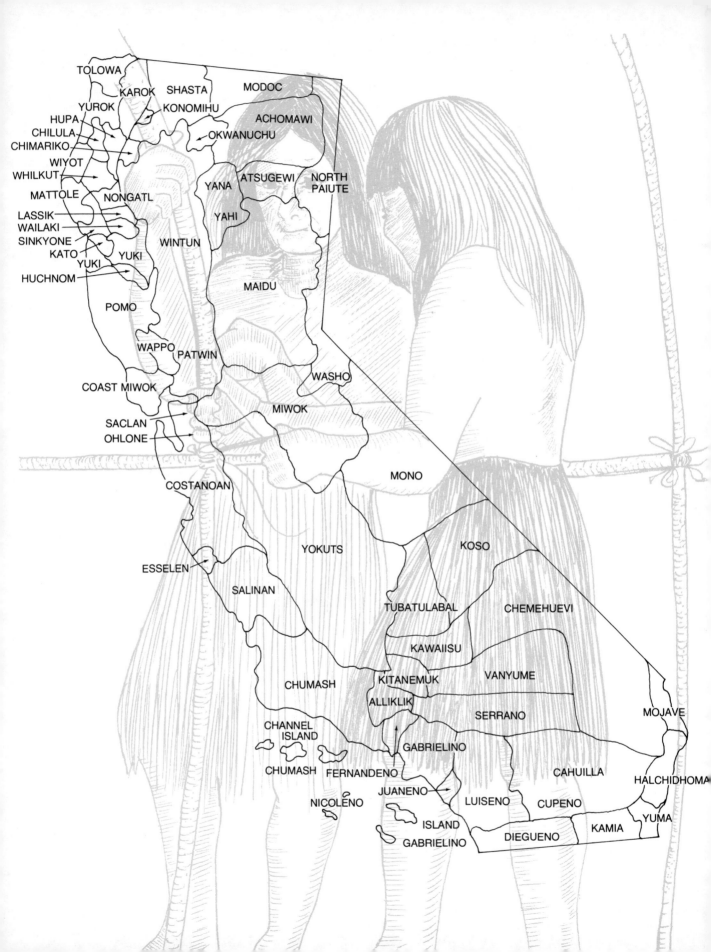

TOLOWA
KAROK
YUROK
HUPA
CHILULA
CHIMARIKO
WIYOT
WHILKUT
MATTOLE
NONGATL
LASSIK
WAILAKI
SINKYONE
KATO
YUKI
HUCHNOM
POMO
WAPPO
COAST MIWOK
SACLAN
OHLONE

SHASTA
KONOMIHU
OKWANUCHU
YANA
YAHI
WINTUN

MODOC
ACHOMAWI
ATSUGEWI
NORTH PAIUTE

MAIDU

PATWIN
WASHO
MIWOK

COSTANOAN

MONO

ESSELEN
SALINAN

YOKUTS

KOSO

CHEMEHUEVI

TUBATULABAL

KAWAIISU
VANYUME

CHUMASH
KITANEMUK
ALLIKLIK
SERRANO
MOJAVE

CHANNEL ISLAND
GABRIELINO

CHUMASH
FERNANDENO
JUANENO
CAHUILLA
HALCHIDHOMA

NICOLENO
LUISENO
CUPENO

ISLAND GABRIELINO
DIEGUENO
KAMIA
YUMA

CHAPTER SEVEN
HOMES OF THE INDIANS

The Indians of California used nature's gifts to build many types of homes. Different types of Indian homes were built depending on the climate and natural resources that were available. Most homes were built so that the entrance faced the south and the back side of the home faced the north or colder side.

PLANK HOMES

In cooler climates of Northern California the Yurok, Hupa, Shasta, Karok and other tribes built their houses from **slabs** of cedar, pine or fir trees from the mountain forests. The wood for plank houses was obtained by burning down trees or using fallen trees. Indians used deer or elk antlers as wedges to split the tree trunks into planks. The Indians dug a pit and built a plank house over it. On the outside, the walls and roof of the house looked low, but on the inside the dug-out floor allowed room for people to stand. The walls and roof were strong and thick. They made family living cool in the summer and warm in the winter.

In the Hupa tribe each family built a **xonta** or plank house. This was their main dwelling where the family ate and the women and children slept. In their xonta each family kept their tools and personal belongings. The xonta could be as large as twenty feet square and was partly built underground. In the middle of the xonta was a sunken living area which was reached by a plank ladder. The main living area was four to five feet beneath ground level and this area was lined with planks like the outside of the house. A fire could be built in the sunken center area of this two-level home for warmth and cooking.

As the Indians entered the doorway of the xonta, there was a storage space above the sunken living area. In this area the Indians stored baskets of dried fish, meat and seeds, wood for the fire and necessary tools.

Near the fire, in the center of the house, the family gathered together. Indian men and special visitors sat farthest from the door, away from any cold drafts that might enter through the doorway. Next to the men sat the women and children. Less important members of the group sat nearest the doorway.

The Hupa men slept in the **sweathouse** or **taikyuw,** also made of planks. It was built similar to a plank house, but it did not have storage areas. The men took sweat baths in the taikyuw. In the afternoons the men lit a fire in the firepit of the taikyuw for a sweat bath. They sat around the fire leaning against carved headrests. When a man finished his bath he dashed to a nearby stream to bathe in the cool waters. Later, he relaxed in the sun, ate with his family and then returned to the taikyuw to smoke, talk, pray and sleep.

Wooden headrests or pillows were used by the Indian men in the sweathouse.

The inside of a plank house

Some Hupa plank buildings have stone foundations which date back thousands of years. The building in the front of this picture is the men's sweathouse. The middle building is the main house used for ceremonies and the house in the back is a family house or xonta. The stone area around the xonta was used by the women as a work area and during warm weather the family often ate there.

BARK HOMES

The mountain tribes such as the Wintun, the Mono and Maidu lived in bark dwellings. Bark dwellings were built by coastal and mountain Indians who could obtain thick slabs of bark from nearby redwood and cedar trees by using elk-horn wedges. These slabs of bark were sometimes piled against a central pole until all holes were covered except a smoke hole in the top and a small doorway down below. Often during cold weather a **portable** door of tule or animal skin was used. A bark dwelling could house a family of six, but during the summer months the Indians lived outside and used their winter dwelling as a storehouse.

BRUSH HOMES

You have learned that Indians of the far north, such as the Yurok, Tolowa, Hupa and Karok tribes, built their homes of planks. You have also learned about the bark houses of the mountain tribes. Indian homes differed depending on geography, climate and materials available.

In the valleys, along the coasts and in the southern desert areas, most homes were built using tules or brush. The **brush house** was round or **oblong** in shape, some were small and some were large. Generally, a pit was dug about two feet deep. Sometimes the pit was round and sometimes it was oblong. The Indians used digging sticks, sharp stones and shells to loosen the soil and baskets were used to remove the soil from the pit. This pit provided a smooth floor for the hut and prevented floor drafts. Next, a frame of willow poles was made to curve over the pit. The frame was then covered with brush or tules that were tied with cord made from nettles, milkweed or hemp fiber. A small opening at the top of the brush hut allowed smoke to escape. If a larger brush **communal** home was planned, an oblong pit was dug and poles were placed in two rows down the long sides of the home to support the long roof. Several families could live in these houses.

These Yokuts children are gathering tule to help build a shelter.

The Yokuts Indian tribes, located in the San Joaquin Valley, were one of the largest Indian groups in California. They built as many as five kinds of brush dwellings. The home most commonly used was the brush house that was built over a two-foot deep pit. When the Spanish expeditions of Fages and Crespi (1772) and Anza and Font (1776) came through the Great Central Valley, they saw many types of brush shelters skillfully built by the Indians. Fortunately, these explorers kept written diaries of what they saw so today we have an accurate description of Indian homes.

A Coast Miwok brush shelter.

One of the most interesting brush houses built by the California Indians was the Yokuts' tule-mat-covered communal house, called a **kawe.** As many as five or six families or a small village could live in a shelter of this kind. In these large dwellings, the Yokuts were aware of each family's privacy. Each family in this kawe had its own living area, firepit and private entrance and did not bother other families' space. These communal dwellings could have been as long as three hundred feet and had a door at each end. It was not considered good manners to walk the length of the house **trespassing** through another person's living space. The Indians were always considerate of one another's territory.

Another type of brush shelter was used only by women or teen-aged girls. This shelter was built over a frame and covered with tules and brush much like a brush house. Its size depended on the number of women living the village and was used by women on special occasions.

In summer, the Indians often built **temporary lean-tos** or flat-topped brush shelters made mainly to keep out the sun. These shelters were used by most Indians in their villages and were also excellent as temporary shelters when some tribes moved into the cooler hills during the warmer months.

A flat-topped brush shelter.

EARTH-COVERED BRUSH HOMES

Throughout California, various tribes of Indians used an earth covering on their brush houses to keep their homes warmer in the winter and cooler in the summer. Some Yokuts Indians of the Great Central Valley built permanent earth-covered brush shelters. Some of these shelters were dug down deeper than the floor of a regular brush hut. This pit helped keep out summer's heat and winter's cold. Often grasses and plants grew on the earth-covered roofs of these shelters and made them blend into the natural **landscape**.

This is the beginning of an earth-covered lodge. A pit was dug and lined with poles to become the framework of the house. Other poles were bent over the upright poles and fastened with nettle or milkweed cord. The tips of the upright poles were pulled together and tied. A hole was left at the top for smoke to escape and tule and brush were laid on top of the framework. A layer of mud several inches thick was applied over the brush or tules.

SWEATHOUSES

Most Indians throughout California built sweat-houses. You have learned that the Indians of Northern California built their sweathouses of wooden planks. Other tribes such as those of the San Francisco Bay Area built sweathouses of brush or brush covered with mud. These sweathouses or **temescals**, as the Spanish called them, were built near a river or stream and usually had a dug-out floor. The walls of the temescal were often covered with a thick layer of mud and the entrance was so small that a man had to be in a crouched position in order to enter.

Some Yokuts of the Great Central Valley called their sweathouse a **mawsh**. The mawsh was oblong and its floor was dug out two or three feet deep. Thick poles were used as a sturdy framework to support a heavy roof made of brush, tules and mud. The roof was low and the entrance was small. As with most Indian tribes, the Yokuts' sweathouse was never more than a short distance from the water and was usually located downstream from the village.

Some Cahuilla Indians of Southern California called their sweathouse a **hash-lish**. They built the hash-lish above ground without a dug-out floor. Four poles were set in the ground about ten feet apart.

Building a hash-lish

Another pole was used to bridge the four poles. The cross pole became the main beam in the sweathouse roof and other poles were leaned against it from all sides to form a tent shaped structure. Brush and mud were packed on the sides and a low opening was left for a door.

Throughout California, sweathouses were commonly used by the men. In a few tribes, however, women were allowed to enter. Maidu women of the North would take their children to the sweathouse. Some Pomo Indians allowed women in their sweathouses at certain times and for special occasions, such as receiving a cure, singing or just observing. Some tribes in California allowed women with **supernatural** powers to enter the sweathouse.

Once or twice daily, the men gathered in the sweathouse. A fire or red hot stones were used to make the Indians sweat heavily. As the house got hotter and hotter, the men began to sweat. They used deer horns to scrape the sweat from their bodies. When the sweat was running off their bodies, they would run outside and jump into a nearby stream.

Some Indians used the sweathouse for games and **initiation** rites. A sweathouse could also be used as a place for treatment of an illness. Sometimes herbs were added to the fire so the fumes would make a pleasant odor and help with the cure.

The Miwok tribe, like many other tribes, used the sweathouse before going deer hunting. They believed that if a man had not sweated, he would not take deer.

Sweating was not necessary for rabbit or mountain lion hunting. Each Miwok man who sweated had a little pile of oakwood to feed the fire. Several men would sweat for two hours and then give up their places to a second group of men. Each man knelt and put his face on the ground so as not to be smothered by the smoke from the fire. The Yuma and Mojave Indians were not known to have used sweathouses.

The interior of a Pomo sweathouse

CEREMONIAL OR DANCE HOUSES

Most Indian tribes throughout California had a village **ceremonial** house which was sometimes called a round house or dance house. This house was the center of many activities.

Some Pomo Indians built large ceremonial houses which were circular in shape. A pit five to six feet deep was dug with fire-hardened sticks and the dirt was carried off to one side to be used later in finishing the roof. The pit was about fifty feet wide and five large posts supported the roof timbers which rose to eighteen feet in height. The roof timbers were covered with brush and the dirt which had been dug out was brought back and packed down on the roof. As many as seven hundred Indians could gather here.

The Yuki Indians built their assembly hall in the same manner—a dug-out pit, dome shaped, covered with brush and then packed with earth. Their earth covered ceremonial houses could hold one hundred to two hundred or more Indians.

Some Cahuilla Indians used a large ceremonial house known as a **kishumnawat.** The kishumnawat was usually circular with a sunken floor. The roof slanted upward from the walls and was supported by forked posts. Willow and other types of brush were used to make the roof.

The ceremonial houses of the Mountain Miwoks were dug into the ground about four to eight feet deep and measured fifty to sixty feet from side to side. The dug-out sides were **reinforced** with large boulders so that the sides of the dance house would not collapse.

Inside the dance house and standing about twenty-five feet apart were four huge tree trunks sunk slightly into the earth dancing floor. The four huge trunks had natural forks or **clefts** at the top of each trunk and these four trunks supported four large logs which were arranged in a square shape. This square shape supported poles which rose to a height of twenty feet from the earth floor.

A Mountain Miwok ceremonial dance house is located in Chaw-se State Park near Volcano, California.

INTERESTING THOUGHTS

Gone are the temescals, granaries, homes and dance houses of the past. Gone are the lived-in plank and bark houses and large communal houses. No more the dash from the sweathouse to the river for a breathtaking dive into cold water. No more the headrests or the gathering of sacred wood for the sweathouse fire. Yet the California Indians have not forgotten their ancestors and how they lived.

Many tribes such as the Mono, Hupa, Paiute and Cahuilla have started museums to preserve valuable baskets and ancient artifacts collected by tribal members and friends. Some tribes such as the Ohlone and Miwok tribes have helped start state or regional parks. These parks help us to better understand how the Indians of the past lived. Other state parks that help us learn about Indian life of the past are located at Sonoma, Millerton Lake and in the Providence Mountains. In these parks, Indian villages are being built so that everyone can see and be a part of our California Indian heritage.

BACKTRACKING

Can you answer these questions?

(1) What are some of the kinds of houses the California Indians built? Tell how they were built and what they looked like.

(2) Where in California would you have found each of the kinds of houses? Why would they be located in these particular areas?

(3) What materials did the Indians use for tools to build their homes?

(4) Why did most of the houses have a hole in the roof?

(5) What kind of Indian home would you like best? Why?

*For Wise Eagles: Why didn't Yuma and Mojave Indians use sweathouses? How would today's **archeologists** know this?

*For Wise Eagles: When you are sick, the doctor tells you to go to bed and stay warm. How would the Indians' practice of heavy sweating and then getting into a cold river be **fatal** as a cure for the white man's **epidemic** diseases, such as smallpox, measles, etc.?

*For Wise Eagles: Why do you think the Indians built sweathouses downstream?

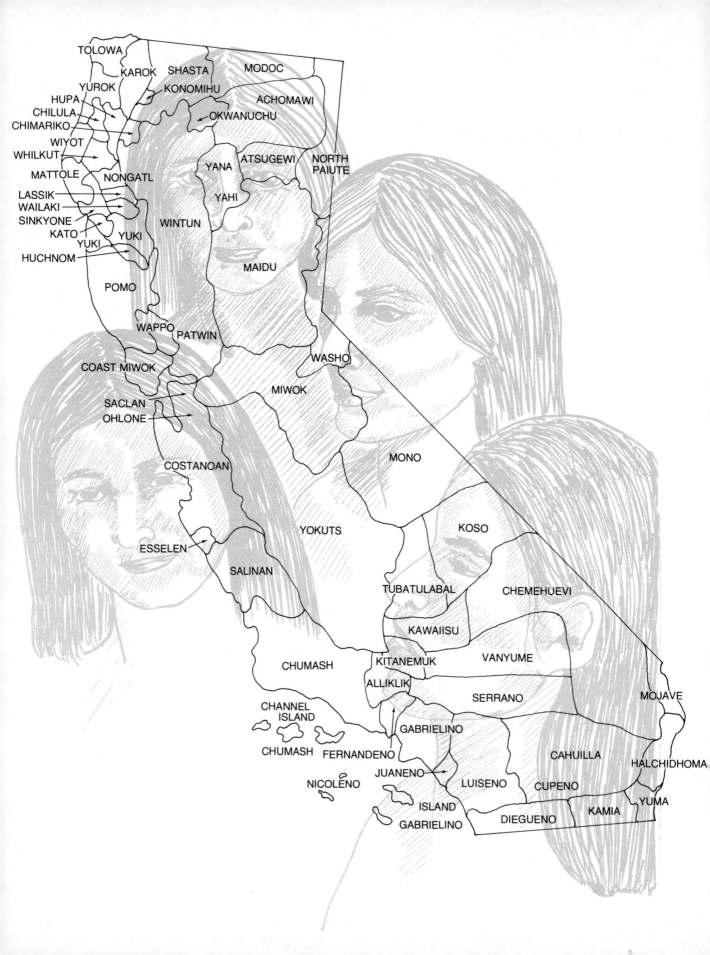

TOLOWA

KAROK

SHASTA

MODOC

YUROK

KONOMIHU

HUPA

ACHOMAWI

CHILULA

OKWANUCHU

CHIMARIKO

WIYOT

YANA

ATSUGEWI

NORTH
PAIUTE

WHILKUT

MATTOLE

NONGATL

YAHI

LASSIK

WINTUN

WAILAKI

SINKYONE

KATO

YUKI

YUKI

MAIDU

HUCHNOM

POMO

WAPPO

PATWIN

COAST MIWOK

WASHO

SACLAN

MIWOK

OHLONE

COSTANOAN

MONO

YOKUTS

KOSO

ESSELEN

SALINAN

TUBATULABAL

CHEMEHUEVI

KAWAIISU

CHUMASH

KITANEMUK

VANYUME

ALLIKLIK

SERRANO

MOJAVE

CHANNEL
ISLAND

CHUMASH

FERNANDENO

GABRIELINO

CAHUILLA

HALCHIDHOMA

JUANENO

NICOLEÑO

LUISENO

CUPENO

YUMA

ISLAND
GABRIELINO

DIEGUENO

KAMIA

CHAPTER EIGHT
CUSTOMS, CEREMONIES AND GAMES

The Indians lived together in **harmonious** groups. They followed strict religious and social rules. There was cooperation among families and early in life each Indian child knew that he was expected to follow certain rules of his tribe, such as respect for family and nature, honesty, patience and love. Indians who could not follow these ways were made **outcasts** of the tribe. An Indian who lost the respect of his tribe also lost his rights to be a member of the family group. Indians depended on one another for food, shelter and protection and so an outcast would find life very difficult.

CHIEFS AND WARFARE

All tribes in California had leaders or chiefs. There were certain men in the tribes who were leaders because of their **influence,** wealth, **reliability** and intelligence.

There were few wars among the Hupa, Yurok and Karok tribes of Northern California. The leaders of these tribes were called upon to settle minor **disputes** in the tribe and to work with neighboring tribal leaders discussing such problems as fishing rights or fair trading. The Modoc, the Achomawi and the Shasta tribes were more involved with **warfare methods**. The Miwok and Wintun chiefs were also **aggressive** and sometimes led their men in invasions of neighboring tribal areas. Wars might start because of dishonest trading, **violating** territorial rights, stealing, kidnapping or raids. After battles, the tribal chiefs were responsible for restoring peace between the tribes. Sometimes dentalium shells, baskets, skins, foods or other goods were used to pay back losses.

When necessary, the Karok Indians wore fighting armor. This picture was taken in the year 1907.

The many Yokuts tribes of the Great Central Valley had a chief for every village. In larger villages there were assistant chiefs who were responsible to the head chief. All chiefs had a special helper or **winatun** whose duty was to greet all travelers, discuss their business and if necessary, take them to the chief. Not only was having a winatun a nice custom, but it allowed the chief time for other important duties. Although there were as many as 35,000 to 50,000 Yokuts living in the Great Central Valley, they respected each other's rights and property, thus, the chiefs had few wars or major problems.

Some Indians living along the Central and Southern coasts of California chose a village chief for his outstanding **valor**. Some of these chiefs had more **authority** than chiefs of other tribes. Chiefs with more authority had helper-chiefs who collected food from the villagers for the head chief. Tribal leaders settled minor disputes in their village. They also settled small **skirmishes** with neighboring tribes so there was little shedding of blood.

The tribes of Southern California had chiefs who **inherited** their positions from **ancestors**. When a chief died, he passed the position on to a son, a brother or a cousin. If a chief had two sons, he had the right to select the son he felt would do the best job, even if his choice was not the oldest son. These Southern tribes, such as the Serrano, Luiseno, Cahuilla, Diegueno and Gabrielino were friendly and were linked by trading and sometimes by marriages. Because of these connections, there was very little **hostility** among the tribes.

The Mojave tribes in the Southeastern section of California had tribal chiefs and some tribes had two or three war chiefs. The Mojave were friendly with neighboring tribes, such as the Diegueno, Cheme-huevi, Kamia and Cahuilla, but they had many wars with the Halchidhoma tribe of the Colorado River area. The Mojave also fought with Arizona tribes.

All chiefs or leaders had to prove themselves as good men or give up the job because of **social pressure**. Indian chiefs were dignified, had courage, were calm under pressure and had wisdom when working with people. The main function of a chief was to bring peace between quarreling families or villages, to organize trading expeditions, to welcome traders to the village, to help direct **ceremonies** and encourage the people to lead more **cooperative** and **productive** lives.

INDIAN DOCTORS AND MEDICINE MEN

Throughout California there were Indian Doctors as well as Medicine Men. An Indian Doctor chanted and danced and used roots, herbs and native plants to make **potions** and cures for sick people. He collected and carried these herbs in pouches or baskets. He tried to cure such illnesses as eye infections, stomach pains, coughs and toothaches. Burns were sometimes healed with leaves from certain plants and ground obsidian was often dusted into the burn. As the burn healed, the leaves were tied on the wound as a **poultice**. Common colds were often cured by the use of teas made from certain native plants, such as wild rose. An Indian Doctor acquired the right to be a doctor by in-heriting the position and buying the special tools or "medicine bundle" that contained necessary articles, such as tiny obsidian points for cutting, dried herbs and roots, small mortars and pestles for grinding, baskets for storage, charmstones, feathers, tobacco and prayer sticks.

These sacred objects were used by an Indian Doctor of the Coast Miwok tribe near Bodega Bay.

Another type of doctor was the Medicine Man, also called a Shaman. He was believed to have **supernatural powers** and acquired these powers from dreams and spirits that entered his body. This Shaman's healing powers would chase bad spirits from a sick person. He **diagnosed** what he believed the sickness to be and sometimes sucked the affected part of the patient's body to remove the poison. When this Shaman cured someone, the Indians believed it was the supernatural spirit within the Shaman's body that did the healing. This type of Shaman was called upon when a person became very ill. He sang, danced and used his supernatural powers to cure the person. If he could not cure a patient, the members of the tribe might try to put the Shaman to death. The people gave the Shaman money or gifts to help cure ill friends and relatives. If a person died, the Shaman had to give back the gifts. If the sick person got well, the Shaman became richer and more important. Sometimes a Shaman became more important than the chief of the tribe. When a Shaman with supernatural powers died, the spirit power left him. His powers could not be passed on to another person.

OTHER TYPES OF MEDICINE MEN

There were other types of Medicine Men or Shaman, such as the Rain or Weather Shaman, the Rattlesnake Shaman and the Bear Shaman.

The Rain Shaman had control over the weather. He would conduct special ceremonies to bring rain or stop flooding. There were more rain doctors in the lower Central Valley and in the southern part of the State than in northern areas. The Yurok, Coast Miwok, Hupa, Karok and San Francisco Bay Area Indians may have had no need for a rain doctor.

The Rattlesnake Shaman was known in various parts of California. He tried to cure or prevent snake bites. Some Shaman, such as those of the Yokuts, had

This is Sinel, a Yokuts Rain Shaman, in his ceremonial costume. The costume is made of eagle down, sparrow hawk feathers, raven feathers and down from a red-tailed hawk. This Shaman was known for his supernatural powers, but his cures were not always successful. The scars on his body show that relatives of the deceased had tried to kill him.

elaborate ceremonies that included the juggling of live rattlesnakes. The Yokuts would not kill a rattlesnake because they believed that the rattlesnake could cause a person to die without striking him. Rattlesnake dances were held throughout the Great Central Valley.

A rattlesnake basket or Tawits was used by Rattlesnake Shaman of the Yokuts tribes. The design on the basket represents the designs of a rattlesnake. Sometimes a Rattlesnake Shaman would put his foot into the basket and if the snake didn't bite, the people would give the Shaman money. After this ceremony, the people believed they would not be bitten by snakes when they went into the fields to gather roots or seeds. The rattlesnake ceremony was repeated each year.

The Bear Shaman was found in most all Indian villages. It was believed that he had the power to turn himself into a grizzly bear so that he could destroy the enemies of the tribe. This Shaman received his power from the very strong and **ferocious** grizzly bear. A Bear Shaman was often feared by tribe members, but the Indians believed that he was a necessary member of the tribe because he could destroy enemies. The Indians of the Great Central Valley and Southern California believed that the Shaman could actually turn himself into a grizzly bear. The Wintun, Pomo and Yuki tribes believed the Bear Shaman had special powers, but that he only dressed in bearskins and was not actually transformed into a bear.

The Rain Shaman and the Rattlesnake Shaman were better known in the southern part of the state. The Bear Shaman was known throughout the entire state from the Shasta Indians to the Diegueno Indians.

BELIEFS AND CUSTOMS

The Indians' lives centered around their families. They followed strict family rules. Each Indian had a daily religious life that included belief in the spirits of rocks, animals and trees. The Indians believed in one Great Spirit that ruled all other spirits. This Great Spirit often took the form of a coyote or eagle.

As you have read in the creation legends in Chapter One, the Great Spirit took the form of Coyote and Eagle to create the world. Throughout California the Indians believed that the creators of the world were animals. Many tribes believed that the eagle and

The grizzly bear is a ferocious animal. Long ago, there were many grizzly bears in California.

Some tribes believed the grizzly bear was an evil spirit and, if killed, the evil spirit would escape. Other tribes such as the Hupa never killed the grizzly bear because they believed that the spirits of grandmothers lived within the bear.

coyote were the creators of the Indians. The eagle was important because he was said to live forever and was a symbol of life after death. The eagle was respected by the Indians and its feathers were used only in special ceremonies.

Coyote was a **cunning,** clever animal and was perhaps more like a person because of his human qualities. Coyote was known for his humor, kindness, generosity, and patience. He was also known to be greedy and **vain.** Coyote was believed to have taught the Indians the correct way to live. The Indians felt great respect for all animals, because each animal was a part of the creation stories that were told over and over again.

Coyote was believed to have taught the Indians the correct way to live.

The Indians believed in good and bad spirits. They felt that the good spirits were always near. The Indians thought that some of the bad spirits went to live in people, and anyone with a bad spirit in them was evil—a witch or devil. They believed devils could turn themselves into animals whenever they wished. Whenever there was trouble or sickness in a tribe, Indians blamed the bad spirits. The Indians were very careful about their personal belongings such as bracelets, necklaces or charms. They never threw a lock of hair away; it was thrown in the fire. They believed that the bad spirit could put an evil curse on that person if the bad spirit came in contact with a lock of hair or broken fingernail, or a personal belonging. Bad spirits caused poor hunting, poor fishing, poor acorn crops and illness.

TOBACCO

A custom of the Indians was smoking tobacco. Indians used several types of tobacco. One of the earliest uses of tobacco leaves was to apply them to the head to relieve headaches. Seeds of these plants were used to **ease** toothaches. Juice from the tobacco plant was put on cuts and sores.

The Indians gathered tobacco when the seeds were ripe, but the leaves were green. They dried and crumbled the leaves for smoking. Tobacco was smoked in pipes. Northern California Indians used a hardwood pipe lined with soapstone while Southern California Indians used stone or clay pipes. The Indians of the Great Central Valley and further south used cane to make pipes.

Some Indians mixed tobacco with **shell lime** and ate it. Tobacco was often used in religious ceremonies. The California Indians did not use as much tobacco as tribes in other parts of the United States.

DEATH

Throughout California the Indians had many customs about death. Death was held in high respect by all the Indians. No one wanted to disturb the spirit of the dead, because the Indians feared that the departed spirit would haunt them. Some Indians did not speak the name of the dead person for one year until a special ceremony was held. Other tribes never mentioned the name of the dead again.

The Indians took care of their dead with special funeral customs. Some tribes **cremated** the dead and some kept the ashes in clay jars or soapstone bowls. A great many tribes buried their deceased in a **flexed** position. In a few cases, Indians placed their dead in branches of trees. These bodies were wrapped in skins and tules and as time went by the bodies slowly **disintegrated** in the hot climate.

Possessions of the dead person were burned or buried with him so he would have them to use in the next world. When the person died, friends and relatives brought gifts to the family. The widow often covered her face with a mixture of charcoal and pine pitch. Some women used asphaltum to paint their faces during **mourning**. In some tribes, during the mourning months, the widow did not bathe or eat meat.

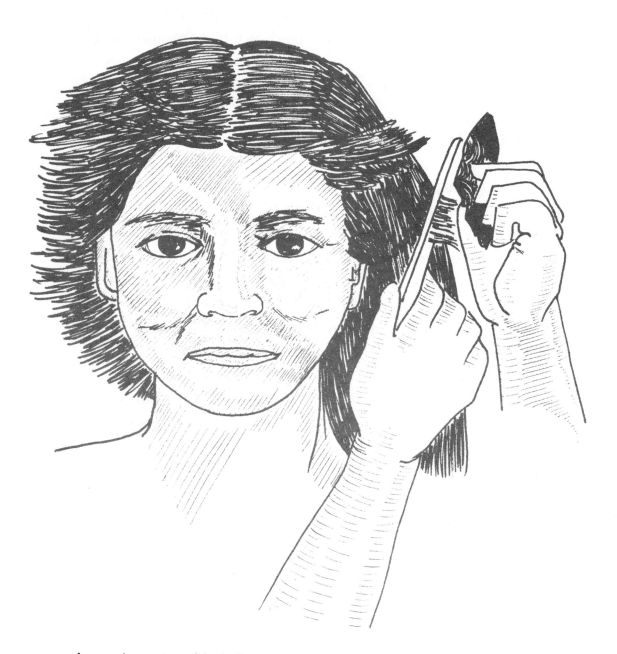

A mourning custom of the Indian women was to burn off their hair. When the hair was burned, it was tightly held between split sticks and singed off with burning bark. The hair that was removed was wrapped around the split sticks and burned. Sometimes the hair was tied to a large stone and tossed into very deep water. By getting rid of her hair in this manner, the Indian knew that evil spirits would not come in contact with her.

CEREMONIES

Indians throughout California had many types of ceremonies. These ceremonies included singing and dancing and often lasted many days. Each ceremony had a special purpose and was passed down from generation to generation by the elders of the tribe. Children watched these ceremonies and sometimes took part in them, and as the children grew up, these ceremonies became a very important part of their lives. Whether the tribe was wealthy or poor, the ceremonies were woven into the hearts and souls of all Indians. You know how important birthday and holiday celebrations are to you, so therefore, you can easily understand the importance of these special ceremonies to the Indians.

MOURNING CEREMONY

The Mourning Ceremony was held by Yokuts of the Great Central Valley and tribes of the South, such as the Gabrielino, Luiseno and Diegueno tribes. This ceremony was held one year after the death and funeral of a person. The Mourning Ceremony was held for all the people of the tribe who had died during the year. The relatives of the dead worked very hard during the months before the Mourning Ceremony making baskets and gathering food. Friends and relatives from nearby tribes were invited and asked to help with the ceremony. The ceremony usually lasted a week. Life-size **images** of each dead person were made

of tule or cattails. These images were elaborately decorated and containers of food and water were placed in
a carrying net on the back of each image for the long
trek into the lands of the Great Spirit. Singing, dancing, crying, praying, story telling and **feasting** took
place and finally the images were burned along with
the last gifts and possessions of the dead. This burning
released the souls of the dead into the spirit world.

The tribes of the North, such as the Pomo, Hupa and
others had a funeral immediately following the death
of a person, but did not have a Mourning Ceremony a
year later. Instead, these tribes remembered the dead
at major ceremonies throughout the year. Perhaps,
during a dance ceremony, an older person would remember a friend or relative and begin weeping.
Others would join in the weeping as they, too, remembered former relatives and friends who had taken part
in this ceremony with them. Thus, a part of some
ceremonies became a time for remembering the dead.

INITIATION CEREMONIES

Two other very important ceremonies that took
place in tribes throughout California were the Boys'
and Girls' **Initiation** Ceremonies. These ceremonies
were like an education because the young people were
given advice and taught the ways of the tribe. These
ceremonies marked the passage of boys and girls from
childhood to adulthood and usually took place when
the children were about twelve or thirteen years old.

BOYS' INITIATION CEREMONY

During the Boys' Initiation Ceremony an older man was appointed or given the job as advisor or protector to one young man. This advisor would be available to advise the boy the rest of his life. Sometimes, another tribal family was asked to help with the Boys' Initiation Ceremonies. In some tribes, jimson weed or angelica was pounded and used in a tea and each boy drank a little of the tea under the watchful eye of his advisor. This tea gave the boys dreams that told of their future lives. During the ceremony, the boys were told the secrets of the universe, the traditions and history of the tribe. Often they were given tests of bravery and courage before their final initiation as an adult member of the tribe.

GIRLS' INITIATION CEREMONY

All Indian tribes throughout California celebrated a growing-up time in young girls' lives. The Girls' Initiation Ceremony was a great event and a time for feasting, singing, dancing and games. The initiation ceremony was attended by friends and relatives and gifts were given. The girls were advised by older women just as the boys had been given advice by older men. The girls were told about the duties of womanhood and special secrets of the universe. Both the Boys' and Girls' Initiation Ceremonies meant that these young people were ready to take their places as young adults in the tribe.

OTHER CEREMONIES

There were many other tribal ceremonies throughout California. Some Northern California tribes celebrated the White Deerskin Dance, the Boat Dance, the Jump Dance and the Brush Dance as well as Eel and Salmon Ceremonies. Some Southern California tribes celebrated Owl and Deer Dances, Eagle Dances and Bird Dances. Many tribes had ceremonies including Spring Ceremonies, Bear and Rattlesnake Ceremonies, Marriage, Birth and Child Naming Ceremonies, Acorn or Agave celebrations as well as other ceremonies celebrating or honoring important events.

The White Deerskin Dance is celebrated every other year in Northern California on the Hupa Indian Reservation. This picture was taken in the year 1903.

INDIAN MUSIC

Indians loved to sing and dance and believed that music would help to keep their village safe from evil spirits. When the Indians sang, they were asking the spirits to be good to them. In their dances, they acted out what they wanted to say to the spirits. Before a hunt, the Indians danced to show the spirits what kind of wild game they needed. They also danced for food or rain. Some dances went on for many days. Men and women enjoyed these dances and the people were always sad when the Indian dancers lay down their costumes.

MUSICAL INSTRUMENTS

California Indians loved music and made musical instruments for their ceremonies. The Northern California Indians did less with musical instruments than the Indians of Southern California. Simple instruments included flutes, whistles, rattles, drums and musical bows. Instruments were made from elderberry wood, bones, reeds, skins, turtle shells, deer hooves and hollow logs.

DRUMS

Some California Indians used foot drums in their musical expression. A foot drum was a large, burned-out log and was usually used in the dance house. The foot drum was very sacred to the Indians. The Hupa Indians used a square drum that was smaller than a foot drum. It was made of a cedar wood frame and wrapped with elk skin.

BULL ROARER

The **bull roarer**, a slat of wood tied to the end of a thong, made a roaring sound when whirled and was used by tribes in the southern part of California. The use of the bull roarer may have been adapted from the Arizona and New Mexico Indians who made use of the instrument in religious ceremonies. Northern California Indians did not usually use the bull roarer.

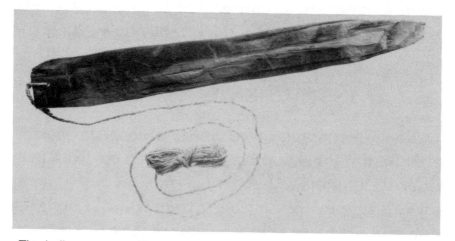

The bull roarer was often used to call the people to a special ceremony.

WHISTLES AND FLUTES

Whistles and flutes were used much more frequently than drums and were made of animal bones, cane or elderberry. Flutes were used in ceremonies and in courting.

The only true musical instrument was an open tube blown across the edge of one end. The desert Indians are known to have blown on tubes with holes in them and were the only California Indians to have played a **fipple** type instrument.

A stringed instrument, like a **Jew's harp**, was used by the Pomo, Maidu, Yokuts and Diegueno Indians. The sound was pleasing and restful and at times was used during **spiritual** ceremonies. Though the flute and harp type instruments were able to carry **melodies**, they were not used in dance ceremonies probably because the sound might have clashed with the singers' voices.

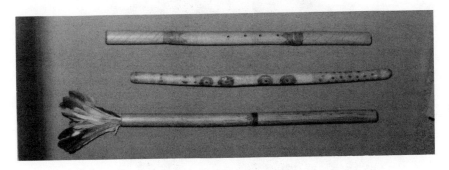

Indian flutes

RATTLES

Every tribe in California used some type of rattle, such as a gravel-filled cocoon bunch rattle, split clap stick or deer-toe rattles. The cocoon rattles were made from dried moth cocoons. Each cocoon was filled with small pebbles and tied to sticks of various lengths. The second type of rattle was a clap stick or split stick about eighteen inches long. The stick was split two-thirds of the way down and tied so it couldn't split anymore. This stick was held in one hand and struck on the palm of the other hand. The third type of rattle, made of deer toes, was used throughout California. The Diegueno Indians of Southern California used the deer-toe rattle as a part of the Mourning Ceremony.

Each rattle was made to be used only once and was burned at the end of the ceremony. Each singer in the Mourning Ceremony made his own deer-toe rattle and only the singers knew how to make them. The gentle clicking of these rattles added a pleasing rhythm to the music of the California Indians.

The Diegueno Indians made deer-toe rattles. The rattles were used only one time and then burned in the Mourning Ceremony. Each rattle used the feet of four or five deer. The deer feet were boiled in water for several hours and then the toes were knocked off and cleaned out with bone tools. Holes were made in the tips of the toes and agave fiber was used to string and knot each toe on a six inch cord. These rattles made a pleasing sound.

GAMES

Everybody enjoys games and the Indians were no exception. When the Indians gathered for ceremonies or celebrations, many types of games were played.

A GUESSING GAME

Indians loved to get together and play guessing games. One of the most popular Indian guessing games was played with two bones—one bone was marked. The game was played with two teams, four or more people on each team. They sat facing each other with a deerskin spread on the ground between them. A pile of counting sticks was placed on the skin to keep score. One player held a bone in each hand and would shuffle the bones from hand to hand behind his back or in front of him. His opponent on the opposite team would then try to guess which hand held the marked bone. Players became expert at changing the bones from one hand to the other and confusing their opponents. Sometimes players chanted and sang to distract the opposing team. If an opponent made a correct guess, his team received a counting stick and the bones went to him to continue the game. This guessing game went on until one team had won all the counting sticks. When one team had all the counters, the game was over. Players and watchers placed bets, used good luck charms and started the game over again. Often this game could go on for days. The rules for this game varied from tribe to tribe.

A STAVES GAME

Another popular game among the Indians was a staves game played by women. Three sticks made from willow or elderberry wood were split in half. Designs were made on the rounded side of the sticks or staves and the split sides were left with no design. Three of the staves had the same design. The other three staves sometimes had a different design. A woman player held her set of staves and threw them like dice on the ground. Players made bets on the way the designs would turn up. Counting sticks were used to keep score.

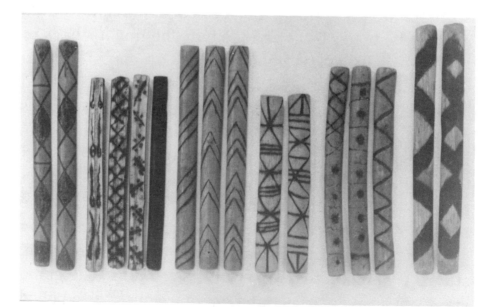

Designs were put on game staves by making a design out of bark and holding the bark against the rounded side of the sticks. The sticks were then held over the fire until blackened with soot so that when the bark was removed the design remained.

A YOKUTS DICE GAME

Indian women also played a dice game. The women skillfully made dice for this game from split shells of the native walnuts or acorn caps. The nut meat was removed from the shells and then each shell was filled with hot pitch or asphaltum. Pieces of abalone shell were pressed into the pitch or asphaltum so that each shell had a different design. Usually the game was played with eight shells and counting sticks were used to keep score. The women of the Yokuts tribes threw the shells onto a large, flat basket tray. The shells were thrown rapidly and points were given depending on how the shells landed—flat side up or flat side down.

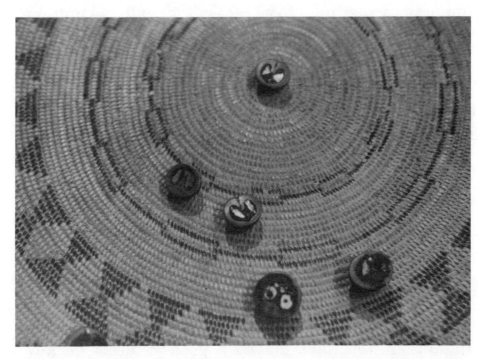

These walnut halves have been filled with pitch or asphaltum and decorated with bright pieces of shell. They were used in a dice game played by women.

SHINNY

Shinny was a game the Indians played much like our hockey. Indian boys learned to play it at a very early age. They often hunted for strong branches with knobs on them to use as shinny sticks and a rounded piece of wood or bone to use as a ball or **puck**. To begin the game, the teams stood in the center of the field and the ball was put into play. Each team tried to make points by hitting the wooden ball past the opposing team's goal line.

INDIANS ENJOYED GAMES

Indians of all ages enjoyed many games and contests. Some of these included hide and seek, tag, broad-jumping, wrestling, foot races, kickball, swimming and diving, string games (cat's cradle) and spinning acorn tops.

Strenuous games, such as shinny were games of strength and **endurance**. These **physical** games were exciting and the players enjoyed the **competition** with each other just as football players today enjoy the thrill of winning a hard fought game. Games of chance, such as guessing games were games of **mental** strength. They involved skill and **dexterity** of the mind and hands. The Indians greatly enjoyed this type of competition.

Many of the games that are played today were played hundreds and hundreds of years ago by the Indians. If you have played a good game of hockey, soccer or football or enjoyed games such as button, button or pick-up-sticks, remember that these are games that began long ago with the native Californians.

A stick and hoop game was played by the Indians and sometimes it was a special game played at the Boys' Initiation Ceremony. A hoop was made from coiled willow branches and sometimes the hole in the hoop was only two or three inches across. Each player had a stick or pole and as the hoop was rolled, the players threw their sticks trying to ring the hole in the hoop. From early childhood, the young Indian boys played the spear and hoop game. This made the boys good spear throwers so that they became skillful fish and game hunters.

INTERESTING THOUGHTS

Can you imagine an Indian ceremony of long ago? You are watching the last rays of the setting sun shine through a forest near a wide peaceful river. It is late summer and the sun flashes long golden rays off the rolling waters as the river gently and quietly flows past an Indian village. The air is warm and all is still. Then, like thunder in the far, far distance, you hear a rumbling, a thumping. The footdrums in the village dance house signal the beginning of a celebration. Gradually the music becomes louder. Now you can hear rattles, whistles and the chanting of voices. Soon dancers appear. Their beautiful costumes are breathtaking. As you watch the rhythmic movement of the dancers, the shells and beads on their skillfully made costumes catch the glow of the sun. The feather headdresses bow and sway ever so gently as the Indian dancers bend forward and back. As evening darkens the land, fires begin to blaze and the figures of dancers are silhouetted against brilliant orange flames. A cool breeze stirs the leaves of the trees, the waters of the river splash gently along the shores and the celebration goes on late into the night.

BACKTRACKING

Can you answer these questions?
(1) Why are ceremonies and customs important to people? Name some ceremonies or customs of your family.
(2) How has medical science progressed since the days of the Indian Doctors and Medicine Men?
(3) What would be your responsibilities in an Indian tribe?
(4) Where did the Indians believe that spirits lived?
(5) Name three types of Indian Doctors or Shaman. Write a paragraph about each.
(6) What is social pressure? How would it work in an Indian tribe? How does social pressure affect our political leaders of today?
(7) Name one or more games that we have today that are "borrowed" from the Indians. How are these games similar to the Indian games?

*For Wise Eagles: Why do you think there were more rain doctors in the lower Central Valley than in the northern parts of California? Check a California map on rainfall and precipitation.

*For Wise Eagles: Why do you think the Southern California Indians used more musical instruments than the Northern Indians?

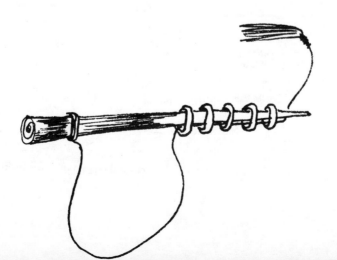

CHAPTER NINE

ISHI, A SPECIAL CALIFORNIAN

ISHI'S EARLY LIFE

Long before the white men came to California, there lived a tribe of Indian people who called themselves Yahi. They lived in the **wilds** east of the Sacramento River between Mill and Deer Creeks. The Yahi were a small group of people, unlike the Yokuts of the San Joaquin Valley or the Pomo of Clearlake who had many, many members in their Indian tribes. The Yahi often fought with neighboring Indian tribes and when they sensed a losing battle, they would retreat to the protection of the Deer Creek wilderness.

Ishi grew up near the cliffs, canyons, mountains and forests between Mill and Deer Creeks. His first awareness of palefaces was when white men overran his village and **massacred** his father and other members of his tribe. The white men blamed the Indians for any difficulties the white settlers experienced. And so, while growing up, Ishi lived in an earth-covered shelter in a hidden village far from white men. Ishi lived with his small family hidden from the sight and knowledge of white men for almost thirty-six years.

ISHI'S INITIATION

When Ishi had seen his twelfth season of the snow, he was initiated into the Yahi sweathouse. Here he learned of the Yahi way of life and the ceremonies and traditions that had been passed down in his tribe from generation to generation. Though his tribe had **dwindled** to only a few members, these traditions were still celebrated as in the past.

Ishi

Each year in the fall, after the acorn gathering, drying of fish and meat, filling and storing of food in handmade baskets for the long winter, Ishi and his family celebrated the harvest season with singing and dancing. At the beginning of the twentieth century, what white man would have guessed that one small group of Indians, supposedly vanished, was still celebrating age old customs.

Ishi and his family loved the animals of the woods and meadows, but in order to survive they hunted deer, rabbit, squirrel and marmot. Ishi fished for salmon and trout in the cool, clear streams during the hot summer months. At this time, Ishi lived in the sweathouse with the other men of the little tribe. In the winter, they lived in his mother's earth-covered shelter. Ishi treasured the memories of these early days. He loved the warmth of the fire and the coziness of the small group as he listened to the tales told by the elders. He would never forget the aroma of the hot bubbling stew and the comforting ways of the older people.

Gradually, life began to change for Ishi. As the small Yahi tribe died one by one, Ishi placed family members and friends in the **ancestral** cave. At each death, he followed the customs of blowing tobacco to the four winds, painting mourning stripes across his face and burning off his hair close to his head. Ishi now found himself alone and tired in his bones and heart. How **wretched** Ishi's life must have been. For three years Ishi wandered without purpose until he was attacked one morning by dogs on a white man's ranch near Oroville, California.

ISHI IN THE WHITE MAN'S WORLD

It was April, in the year 1911, when Ishi came into the white man's world. He was found **crumpled** against the side of a **slaughterhouse**. He had no knife nor bow and arrows. After spending the night in the Oroville jail, Ishi was introduced to a man named A. L. Kroeber. Dr. Kroeber took Ishi to San Francisco to live. He showed Ishi many Indian **artifacts**, some of which had belonged to Ishi's very own tribe. Here, in this new world, Ishi discovered that there were both good and bad white men like there were good and bad Indians.

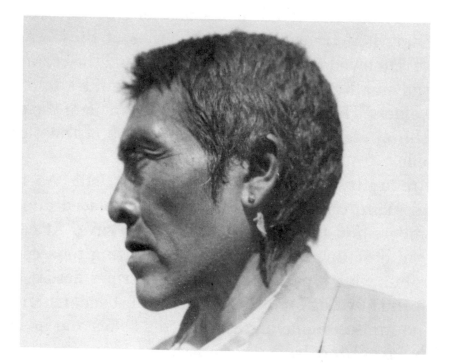

Ishi was in mourning for the loss of his loved ones when he was found in Oroville, California in 1911. The people who found him gave him clothing.

Ishi learned to wear clothes of the white man, but never shoes! He shook hands to greet new friends even though this was not his custom. He was not impressed by the tall buildings of San Francisco because he probably compared them in his mind to the lofty **crags** and cliffs of the Yahi world where he had grown up. Although Ishi thought that modern inventions such as the automobile, airplane and trolley car were truly **miracles**, what really impressed him were the **throngs** of people in the city of San Francisco. Never had Ishi seen so many people in one place before! He was constantly **awed** and large crowds frightened him.

A RETURN TO YAHI COUNTRY

During the five years that Ishi lived in San Francisco, he made one trip back to the Yahi world with Dr. Kroeber and three friends. The men lived as Ishi had lived—hunting with bows and arrows, fishing, taking sweat baths, gathering berries and seeds. This they did for over a month. On this trip, the white men gained a better understanding and a lasting appreciation for the Indian way of life.

Ishi making a bow

Ishi showing how to use a bow and arrow

Ishi skinning a deer

INTERESTING THOUGHTS

When Ishi died, the world lost a special individual—a man of courage, love and gentleness. Ishi helped to bridge a new understanding between the white man's world and the Indian world. By living and talking with Ishi, many white men came to understand the spirit that lives within the Indian—a spirit that is quiet, patient, kind and sensitive to the world about him.

BACKTRACKING

Can you answer these questions?

(1) Where did Ishi grow up? Can you pinpoint this spot on a California map?

(2) How did Ishi and his family survive without being discovered for so many years?

(3) Ishi lived thirty-six years hidden from the white man's world. Gradually his life began to change. Why did his life change and how did his life change?

(4) Why did Ishi leave his mountain home and enter the white man's world?

(5) What impressed Ishi the most about the white man's world? Why did these things impress him more than others?

(6) Did Ishi's life with Dr. Kroeber help him to better understand the white man's world? How did it help?

(7) Does Ishi's life help you to better understand the life of the California Indian? Why?

*For Wise Eagles: Read the book **Ishi, Last of his Tribe** by Theodora Kroeber. Write or give an oral book report to your class. Illustrate your report with colorful pictures.

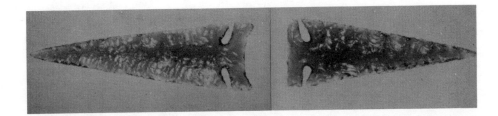

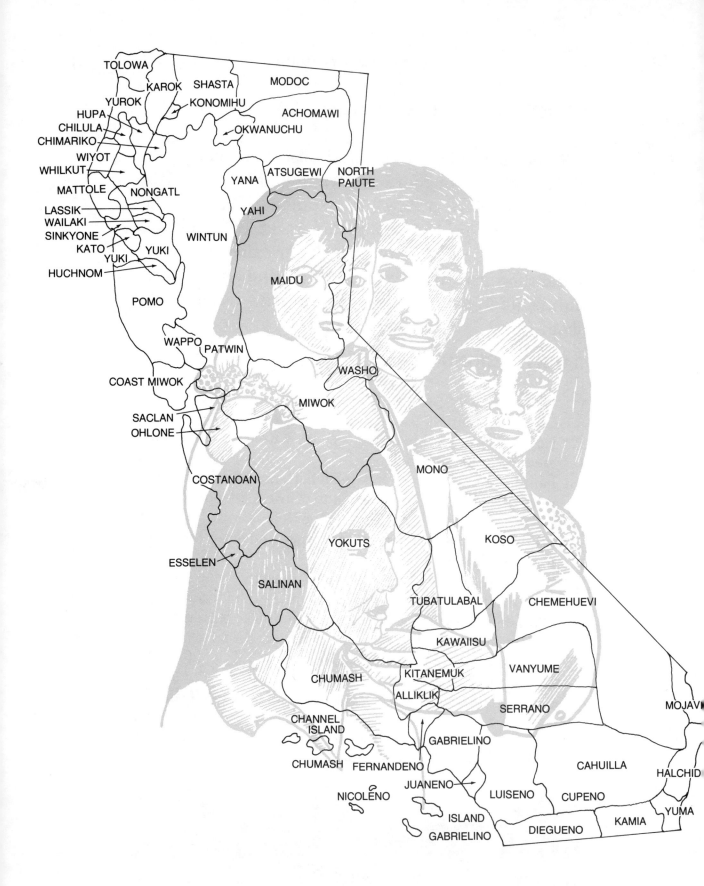

CHAPTER TEN
CALIFORNIA INDIANS THEN AND NOW

Thousands of years ago nature whispered its welcome to the first Californians. The Indians accepted the warmth of this greeting and lived in the beauty of the canyons, hills and deserts of California. The Indians lived in harmony with nature and knew that this land would be a part of them forever.

As the centuries passed, the Indians walked the lands of California. The earliest Spanish expeditions in California followed the Indian trails and as the Spanish explored this new land, they claimed all rivers, lakes, deserts and mountains for Spain. The first explorers did not stay or settle these lands. The Indians were not disturbed by these early explorers and the Indians' way of life continued as it had for centuries. Little did the Indians know that these brief encounters with the Spanish would soon change their lives and their peaceful existence with nature.

SPANISH PADRES

As the first Spanish **padres** arrived in California, the Indians' lives began to change. The padres came as **missionaries** to share their God with the Indians. They wanted to show the Indians how to live, eat and dress like Europeans, how to farm and how to pray to the Christian God.

For over fifty years the mission padres tried to teach the Indians their way of life, according to Spanish custom. The padres felt that if the Indians stayed with them as **apprentices** for ten years, the Indians would then be educated enough to teach other Indians a new way of life. Some of the Spaniards caused the Indians great unhappiness and gradually, the Indians grew to dislike mission life. The Spanish way of life stayed on in California, but it was not passed on by the Indians.

Soon the Mexican flag flew over the land and most of the missions were sold or abandoned. The Indians were given land by the Mexicans and were left to adapt to another change.

MORE CHANGES

As more people came to California to live, they brought with them many diseases such as mumps, chickenpox, **influenza** and **diphtheria**. The Indians had no **natural immunity** to these new diseases. **Severe epidemics** began and complete tribes of Indians died out. Between 1770 and 1910 there were 133,000 Indians living in California, but by the year 1910 there were less than 16,000 Indians.

Americans entered California by the thousands when gold was discovered in the late 1840's. The Indians were faced with people eager to take land and life, regardless of **human rights**. Miners flooded into California and took the Indians' lands. Many Indians fled to the **remote** hill areas, while others remained in the mining settlements to survive as best they could.

THE BUREAU OF INDIAN AFFAIRS

When the Constitution of the United States was adopted in the year 1788, the thirteen original states gave the federal government the responsibility of working with Indian tribes. The men in the United States government who worked with the Indians were called the War Department. In 1824 the men in this department decided to name their group the **Bureau of Indian Affairs**. Many years after that, the Bureau of Indian Affairs became a part of the **Department of the Interior** of the United States government and remains in this department to this day.

The Bureau of Indian Affairs is headed by a commissioner who is appointed by the President of the United States with the **consent** of the **United States Senate**. If an Indian wishes to have the services of the Bureau of Indian Affairs, he or she must live on a reservation or must have Indian heritage from a tribe or group of Indians recognized by the government of the United States.

INDIANS TODAY

Many California Indians live on **reservations**, land granted to them by the government of the United States. Reservations are areas of land reserved for Indian use. Every active reservation in California has a governing body. The governing body of the tribe is generally referred to as the **tribal council** and is made up of men and women elected by the vote of the adult members of the tribe and ruled over by the **tribal chairperson** or **spokesperson**. The tribal council elected in this way has the authority to speak and act for the tribe and to represent the tribe in dealings with federal, state and local governments.

There is also land in California that is owned by groups of Indians. The Indians **pool** their money and buy their own land. The government does not own this land. These **parcels** of land are called **rancherias**.

The traditions and ways of the past play an important part in everyone's life. The California Indians today preserve their traditions by teaching their children the history, customs, songs, dances and ceremonies that have been passed down from generation to generation.

Many tribes throughout California hold special gatherings during the year. Several years ago, the native Californians held a gathering of their people where some of their traditional customs, legends, dances and songs were shared. This has become an annual event and is held at Cal-Expo in Sacramento during September. It is called "California Indian Days".

At a "California Indian Days" celebration, these young girls took part in traditional dances. As the young people danced, an elder of the tribe spoke: "We are proud these children are doing these dances. We want them to know where they came from, who they are and then, they in turn, when they go to school outside, can pledge themselves to the world to deal with the modern world also."

The songs of these men tell the stories of the Indians' travels in ancient times.

The Fort Mojave Tribal Band represents the Mojave tribe located near the town of Needles.

These bird singers are from the Morongo Indian Reservation, the Palm Springs Indian Reservation and the Torres-Martinez Indian Reservation in Southern California.

These children are learning the ways of their tribes through song and dance. The ways of the ancients are a part of the children's heritage.

An elder of the tribe told the audience: "We want our children to know of their ancestors."

The elder continued: "This is what we are trying to give our children so they will know of their heritage."

The Indians of today enjoy the games of the past.

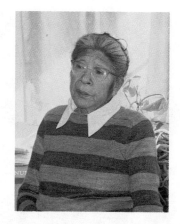

The Malki Museum is Southern California's first all Indian museum. It is located on the Morongo Indian Reservation near Banning. Jane Penn, a Wanikik Cahuilla Indian, started this museum with the help of many people. This museum brings pride to the hearts of the Indian people.

Ed Mata, a Yokuts Indian tells stories of his people to school children and at public gatherings. He enjoys telling Indian stories that teach lessons to live by. He talks about the beauty in all people and encourages his listeners to find good in every human being.

Mrs. Loretta Head, a Pomo Indian, has shared the heritage of her people with family, friends and classroom students. She is shown here with her grandchildren Terry (left), Joe and Noreen DiMaggio and one of her daughters, Nancy DiMaggio (right). Nancy is proud of her Indian heritage. She remembers the times that she spent with her grandmother on a rancheria near the Russian River. They fished in the Indian way, made acorn mush and black bread. During the mushroom season, Nancy and her grandmother hunted for giant mushrooms—one of Nancy's fondest memories. The Indian traditions and customs that Mrs. Head is sharing with her family will always be a special part of their lives.

Major cities throughout the state usually have an Indian center which serves as a general informational services center as well as a meeting place for the urban Indians.

Rachel Ann Joseph Bluestone, a Shoshone-Paiute-Mono Indian, is the American Indian coordinator in the Office of the Governor, Sacramento. Ms. Bluestone's responsibilities are to help protect the rights of American Indians under both state and federal law and to make sure that American Indian residents are receiving all monies and services to which they are entitled. Ms. Bluestone and the legislators of California address the issues affecting California's Indian population.

Andrew Andreoli, a Hupa Indian, is a consultant for the State Department of Education. He was born on the Hupa Reservation. He speaks to many groups about Indian education and coordinates Indian programs with public schools.

INTERESTING THOUGHTS

From the beginning, the Indians have been a part of the first whispers of California. Their heritage touches the dawning of a new world. The ancestors of the Indians today were the first people to hear the whisperings of nature as they walked among the grasses and wildflowers of the California hills and valleys. These first Californians respected the land and all that the Great Spirit had given to them. They lived in harmony with nature and their lives sent roots deep into the warmth of the California soil. Because of these strong roots, the Indians were able to survive many changes and like the mighty oak, new generations have grown to teach us the ways of the past.

All Californians should learn the ways of the Indians. We are grateful to the Indians for their respect of our natural resources. Now, like the Indians, we must learn to appreciate and preserve the environment for future generations of Californians.

BACKTRACKING

Can you answer these questions?

(1) Why did epidemic diseases such as mumps, chickenpox, etc. cause a great decline in the population of the Indians? Do we have epidemic diseases today?

(2) How was the Bureau of Indian Affairs started? How does it help Indians today?

(3) How are reservations governed today? Discuss the duties of the tribal council and tribal chairperson.

(4) What is a rancheria? How does it differ from a reservation?

(5) Why is it important to learn about family traditions? How do you learn about your family traditions?

(6) In what ways have the California Indians contributed to our lives today?

CREDITS

— American Museum of Natural History, Central Park West, N.Y. 10024. Photo page 126

— Chaw-se State Park. Photo page 38 by Terry Olson, Alamo, Ca. 94507. Page 153, 154 by Allen Faber, Danville, Ca. 94526

— Frank F. Latta, Bear State Books, Santa Cruz, Ca. 95061. Photo page 111 (bottom), 145, 148, 163

— Hoopa Indian Reservation. Photo page 143, 206 by Michele Lasagna

— Humboldt County Office of Education, N.I.C.E. Program, P.O. Box 1408, Eureka, Ca. 95501. Legends page 2–4, 44–45, 87–88, 94

— Loretta Head, Alameda, Ca. Photo page 107

— Lowie Museum of Anthropology, University of California, Berkeley, Ca. 94720. Photo page 20, 90 (bottom), 93, 97, 106, 108 (top), 109 (bottom), 118 (top), 120, 134, 142, 151, 158, 161, 164, 174, 176, 180, 190, 191, 192, 193

— Morongo Indian Reservation, Malki Museum, 11–795 Fields Road, Banning, Ca. 92220. Photo page 38 (top), 111 (top)

— Miwok Indian Village. Point Reyes, Ca. Photo page 146, 147 by Michele Lasagna

— Naturegraph Publishers Incorporated, P.O. Box 1075, Happy Camp, Ca. 96039. Legends page 5–6

GLOSSARY

This glossary gives the meanings of words only as they are used in this book. You may wish to use a dictionary to find other meanings for these words.

abundant: in plentiful supply; more than sufficient.

acorn: the fruit of the oak tree, consisting of a thick-walled nut usually set in a woody, cuplike base.

adze: an axlike tool with an arched blade at right angles to the handle, used for dressing wood.

agave: a fleshy-leaved tropical American plant. The leaves are used for food and fiber.

aggressive: showing a readiness to attack others; ready to fight.

ailment: a sickness.

ancestor: a person from whom another person is descended; a person far back in one's family; ancestral.

ancient: of existing, or occurring, in the times long past.

apprentice: a person who must work for another for a certain length of time in return for instruction in a trade, art or business.

archeological sites: a place or plot of land where evidence of man's life and culture in past ages has been studied.

archeologist: one who studies archeology.

archeology: the study of man's life and culture in the past ages.

area: a part of the earth's surface; region.

arrowhead: the pointed, removable striking tip of an arrow.

arrowshaft: the slender stem of an arrow.

artifact: an object produced or shaped by human workmanship; especially a simple tool, weapon or ornament of archeological or historical interest.

artisan: a person skilled in making a particular product; craftsman.

asphaltum: a thick, dark-colored substance obtained from natural beds or from certain petroleums.

aspirin: a white drug made from salicylic acid used for relief of pain and fever.

authority: power to influence or command thought, opinion or behavior.

awe: to be influenced or inspired by someone or something.

awl: a pointed tool for making holes, as in wood or leather.

barb: a sharp point pointing in the opposite direction from the main point of a weapon or tool, as on an arrow, fishhook or spear.

Bering Strait: a strait (narrow passage) between Alaska and the Soviet Union in Asia, connecting the Bering Sea and the Arctic Ocean.

botanist: one who studies botany.

botany: the study of plants.

bough: a large branch of a tree.

boulder: a large, rounded stone block lying on the surface of the ground, or sometimes embedded in the soil.

bountiful: abundant, plentiful.

buoyancy: the ability to float in a liquid or to rise in air or gas.

buoyant: having buoyancy.

brush house: a round or oblong shaped home made from tules or brush.

bull roarer: a slat of wood tied to the end of a thong which makes a roaring sound when whirled.

burden: something that is carried; a load.

Bureau of Indian Affairs: a department in the U.S. Federal Government that works with Indians.

cedar: any of several cone bearing evergreen trees of the genus cedrus.

ceremonial: related to ceremony.

ceremony: an act or series of acts performed in some regular order, as required by ritual or custom.

chafe: to become worn or sore from rubbing.

chert: a hard stone with a waxlike luster that comes in colors of blue, gray, green and red.

Christopher Columbus: an Italian navigator in the service of Spain; opened the New World to exploration.

cinnabar: a red ore.

citric acid: of or obtained from citrus fruits or by fermentation of sugars and used as a flavoring.

civilization: a group of people living in an organized way.

cleft: a crack; crevice; split.

communal: of or concerning a commune.

commune: a small community whose members have common interests and in which property is often shared or owned by more than one person.

communicate: to express oneself in such a way that one is readily and clearly understood.

competition: a contest between rivals; the act of competing.

consent: approval of what is done or proposed by another.

continent: one of the six or seven great land masses on the globe.

cooperative: a willingness and ability to work with others.

courting: attempting to gain affection or love.

crag: a steeply projecting mass of rock forming a part of a rugged cliff or headland.

creation: to make or begin something; to bring into existence.

creation legend: a story handed down from earlier times concerning creation.

cremate: to reduce to ashes by means of fire or great heat.

crumple: to crush together or press into wrinkles; rumple.

custom: a tradition; a special way of doing something.

cunning: exhibiting skill; sly.

dau: a break or change in a pattern.

deceased: dead; recently dead.

deciduous: shedding or losing foliage at the end of growing season; not permanent.

delicacy: something exceptionally pleasing and appealing, especially a choice food.

dentalium: any of a genus of widely distributed tooth shells; shells that look like long teeth.

Department of the Interior: a department of the U. S. Federal Government that deals with the conservation and development of the natural resources of the United States.

deplete: to use up or exhaust.

dexterity: skill and ease in using the hands.

diagnose: to recognize by its symptoms, as a disease, to make a diagnosis.

diphtheria: a disease with fever in which the air passages become coated with a soft membrane that stops breathing.

disc: any thin, flat, circular plate.

disguise: to change the manner or appearance of in order to prevent recognition.

disintegrate: to separate or break up into small pieces.

dispute: an argument; a debate; a quarrel.

double bladed paddle: a pole with a paddle at either end.

drought: a long period with no rain, especially during a planting season.

dug-out: a boat or canoe made by hollowing out a log.

dwindle: to become steadily less until little remains.

ecologist: one who studies ecology.

ecology: the study of living things and their relationship to the environment.

edible: capable of being eaten; nonpoisonous.

elaborate: worked out with great care or much detail.

elder: an older, influential person of a family, tribe or community.

endurance: the ability to withstand hardship or stress.

epidemic: spreading widely and affecting large numbers of people at the same time.

erected: to raise upright; set on end; lift up.

excavate: to uncover by digging.

exploration: an investigation or search.

fast: to restrain or abstain from eating all or certain foods.

fatal: causing death; as a fatal accident or injury.

feast: an elaborate meal often accompanied by a ceremony or entertainment.

ferocious: fierce, savage, cruel, threatening.

fiber: a tough substance or tissue, such as raw wool, cotton or silk, the threadlike parts of which can be separated and spun into thread or yarn.

fibrous: having, consisting of, or resembling fibers.

fipple: a wooden block that forms a channel through which air can travel at the mouth-end of certain musical wind instruments.

flex: to bend easily; capable of being bent; not stiff; flexible.

flint: a very hard, fine-grained quartz that sparks when struck with steel.

foreshaft: the front section or part of a spear or arrow.

framework: a structure for supporting or enclosing something.

garment: any article of clothing.

generation: a group of individuals (who lived more or less at the same period of time) with the same cultural or social backgrounds.

geography: a science that studies the natural features of the earth such as climate, mountains, rivers, etc.

geology: the study of the history and structure of the earth.

geomorphology: the study of land forms.

granary: a building for storing acorns.

graphite: soft, black carbon used in making pencil lead.

gruel: a thin, watery mush or porridge.

gum: a sticky substance from certain plants and trees.

harmonious: being in agreement or harmony.

hashlish: a Southern California Cahuilla Indian sweathouse.

hemp: a fiber from various plants.

heritage: that which comes or belongs to one by reason of birth.

hostility: unfriendliness; ill will.

human rights: that which belongs to anyone by just claim, legal guarantees, moral principles.

igneous: something formed from the heat within the earth.

image: a copy, reproduction or imitation of the form of a person or thing.

immunity: the ability to resist a disease.

India: a country in Southern Asia.

influence: power from wealth, position or character.

influenza: a disease with inflammation of the respiratory tract, fever, muscular pain and irritation in the intestinal tract.

ingenious: clever; having the ability to solve problems; skillful.

inhabitant: a permanent resident in a place.

inherit: to receive from a parent or ancestor; to receive by birth.

initiation: the ceremonies or instructions with which one is made a member of a society or group; to admit to a club or society by special ceremonies.

inlaid: set into a surface in a decorative pattern.

instep: the arched middle part of the human foot in front of the ankle joint.

intricate: complicated; having many parts.

jasper: a variety of quartz, reddish, brown or yellow in color.

Jew's Harp: a small lyre-shaped instrument that when placed between the teeth gives tones from a metal tongue struck by the fingers.

juniper: a low evergreen shrub or tree with a blue berrylike fruit.

kawe: a Yokuts tule-mat-covered communal house.

kernel: a grain or seed, as of a cereal grass, enclosed in a hard husk.

kidney: one of a pair of glands located in the lower back near the spine that discharges in liquid form the waste products from the body.

kishumnatwat: a Cahuilla ceremonial house.

kitcateratc: a Serrano Indian tule covered house.

landscape: a view of scenery on land.

lattice: an open framework made of strips of metal or wood.

latticework: a lattice or something resembling a lattice.

lava: hot, melted or molten rock that issues from a volcano or a fissure in the earth's surface.

leach: to drain a liquid through a material to remove an undesirable substance.

lean-to: a flat-topped brush shelter made mainly to keep out the sun.

legacy: something handed down from an ancestor or predecessor or from the past.

legend: a popular story handed down from earlier times.

limpet: a marine mollusk that has a tent-shaped shell and sticks to rocks of tidal areas.

loin cloth: a piece of deerskin hung front and back from the waist by a strip of leather called a thong.

luster: sheen; gloss.

magnesite: a white, yellowish or brown crystal mineral.

mammal: a member of a class of vertebrate animals, including man with self-regulating body temperature, hair and in the females, milk-producing glands.

marrow: a soft tissue that is found in the inside of bones.

massacre: to kill a large number of people.

mature: to bring to full development; ripen.

mawsh: a Yokuts (from the Great Central Valley) sweathouse made from thick poles for the framework, and brush, tules and mud for the roof and walls.

medicinal: healing, curative; having the power to cure a disease.

melody: in music, a series of tones arranged to make a pleasing effect; the leading part in a song; a tune.

mental: having to do with the mind; carried on in the mind.

mesquite: a spiny tree or shrub native to Southwestern United States.

midden: an area where refuse or unneeded materials are piled.

milkweed: a slender plant two to five feet tall with long narrow leaves. The stems have a milky juice when crushed.

miracle: an event that cannot be explained by any law of nature.

missionary: one who is sent on a mission; especially a person sent to do religious work in some territory or foreign country.

moccasin: a soft, heelless shoe made of leather.

monumental: enormous, astounding or outstanding.

mortar: a bowl-like container made of a hard material in which substances are crushed or ground with a pestle.

mourning: the act of feeling sorrow for some loss.

mourning ceremony: a ceremony held one year after the death and funeral of a person.

narcotic: a drug that in moderate doses dulls the senses, relieves pain and induces profound sleep.

natural: present in or produced by nature; not artificial or manmade.

natural resource: the natural wealth of a country, consisting of land, forests, mineral deposits, water, etc.

navigate: to control the course of a ship or aircraft.

nettle: a plant having toothed leaves covered with hairs that secrete a stinging fluid that affects the skin on contact.

nourishment: that which supports life and growth in a living organism; food.

oak gall: a fungus that sometimes grows on the oak tree that could be pounded into a powder and used as a wash for the eyes or open sores.

oblong: longer than broad, with parallel sides; rectangular.

obsidian: an acid resistant, lustrous volcanic glass, usually black or banded and displaying curved, shiny surfaces when broken.

olivella: a type of seashell.

olla: a large, bulging wide-mouthed jar with looped handles.

outcast: a person who is cast out or expelled, as from home or country.

padre: father; used as a title of address for a priest in Spain.

paralyze: to make helpless or unable to move.

parcel: a tract or plot of land.

patience: the capacity of calm endurance and self-control.

pestle: a club-shaped hand tool for grinding or mashing substances in a mortar.

physical: of or pertaining to the body, as distinguished from the mind or spirit; bodily; physically.

pine nuts: seeds or nuts from the pinecone of the pine tree.

pinyon: any of several pine trees bearing edible, nutlike seeds.

pitch: the resin or the sap of various trees, such as the pines.

plumbiferous: containing lead.

poisonous: containing poison.

pole: to propel a boat, raft or similar watercrafts with a pole.

pollen: the yellow dustlike particles in small seed plants that fertilize the seeds.

pool: to put (interests, money, etc.) into a common stock or fund, as for a financial venture, according to agreement.

portable: capable of being carried; easily moved.

potion: a liquid mixture or dose.

poultice: a moist, soft mass of bread, meal, clay or other adhesive substance, usually heated, spread on cloth and applied to warm, moisten or stimulate an aching or inflamed part of the body.

prey: any creature hunted or caught for food.

procedure: the way any business or action is carried on.

productive: producing abundantly; fertile.

prong: a slender projecting part, as a point of an antler. A sharply pointed part of a tool or instrument.

puck: a piece of wood or bone used as a ball in the game "shinny."

pumice: a porous lightweight volcanic rock used in solid form as an abrasive and in powdered form as a polish.

quiver: a case for carrying arrows.

radioactive: sending out energy in the form of rays.

radiocarbon: radioactive carbon.

rancheria: a small ranch.

reinforce: to give more force or effectiveness to; strengthen; support.

reliable: trustworthy.

remedy: a medicine or any form of treatment that cures or relieves.

remote: located far away; relatively distant in space.

repellent: a substance used to drive off insects.

reputation: recognition by other people of some characteristic or ability; as, to have the reputation of being an honest person.

reservation: land granted to the Indians by the United States government.

responsibility: a thing or person that one is responsible for; obligation.

rheumatism: a disease in which there is stiffness in the muscles and joints, making movement painful.

rhythm: in music, a flow of sound marked by accented beats coming at regular intervals.

rhythmic: showing rhythm.

rite: a ceremony conducted according to a fixed rule.

rodent: any of various mammals, such as a mouse, rat, squirrel or beaver, characteristic of having large incisors adapted for chewing or nibbling.

route: a road, course, or way for travel from one place to another.

rush: a grasslike marsh plant.

sacred: made or declared holy.

salicylic: a white crystalline acid used in making aspirin, as a preservative and flavoring agent.

scientific: broadly having or appearing to have an exact, objective, factual, systematic basis.

scientific theory: a theory or hypothesis based on a scientific approach.

scorch: to burn slightly so as to alter the color or taste.

scraggly: ragged; irregular; untended or unkempt.

scrub: a thick growth of small or stunted shrubs or trees.

severe: strict or very serious.

shell lime: a white powdery substance, containing calcium, made from shells.

siphon: to draw off or convey through.

site: the place or plot of land where something was, is, or is to be located.

skim: to remove floating matter from a liquid.

skirmish: any minor conflict or dispute.

slab: the outside piece, with or without the bark, taken from a log in sawing it into boards.

slaughterhouse: a place where animals are butchered.

slingshot: a Y-shaped stick with an elastic strap attached to the prongs, used for flinging small stones.

snare: a trapping device, often consisting of a noose, used for capturing birds and small animals.

snuggly: comfortably sheltered from the cold and the weather; cozy.

soapstone: a soft stone having a soapy feel and composed mostly of talc, chlorite and often some magnetite.

social pressure: being forced by others to do something.

soggy: saturated with moisture; soaked.

spiritual: having to do with man's spirit or soul.

spiritualism: the view that the spirit is a prime element of reality.

spleen: an organ near the stomach or intestine of most vertebrates.

spokesperson: a person who speaks for a group.

spoor: a track or trail, especially that of a wild animal pursued as game.

stalking: tracking game or wild animals.

staple: a major commodity grown or produced.

stoke: to tend a fire or furnace.

strenuous: vigorously active; calling for energy or stamina.

substituted: put or use in place of another.

succulent: full of juice.

supernatural: having to do with something beyond or outside of nature.

supple: not breaking or creasing when bent; flexible.

sweathouse: a place to live in for several days and nights to sweat, fast, smoke and dream.

taikyuw: a sweathouse made by some Northern California Indians.

tanned: the process in which hides are made into leather by soaking in tannin.

tannic acid: a substance made by the oak tree and found in acorns.

tattoo: a permanent mark or design made on the skin.

temescal: a San Francisco Bay Area tribe sweathouse made of brush or brush covered with mud.

temporary: lasting for a time only; not permanent.

terrain: a tract of land; ground.

thatch: a roof or covering, as for a house or hut, made of straw, reeds or rushes.

theory: a hypothesis; the analysis of a set of facts in their relation to one another.

thicket: a thick growth of underbrush.

thirst quencher: something that quenches, or satisfies one's thirst.

thong: a narrow strip of leather or other material used for binding or lashing.

throng: a large group of people gathered or crowded closely together.

throwing stick: a stick that is thrown; often having a sharp point.

tinder: easily burned material, such as dry twigs, used to kindle fires.

tobacco: a tall, erect year around herb cultivated for its leaves.

trading: to make an exchange of one thing for another.

tradition: the handing down of information, beliefs and customs by word of mouth or by example from one generation to another without written instruction.

trek: a slow journey.

trespass: to go onto another's property unlawfully; a trespasser is one who trespasses.

tribal chairperson: one who rules over the tribal council; spokesperson.

tribal council: the governing body of the tribe made up of men and women elected by vote of the adult members of the tribe.

tribe: any of various systems of social organization comprising several local villages, bands, districts, lineages or other groups and sharing a common ancestry, language, culture and name.

tripod: a three-legged utensil, stool, table or object.

tump line: a strap slung across the forehead or the chest to support a load carried on the back.

turban: a type of seashell.

United States Senate: the upper and lower houses in the legislature of the United States. The Senate takes part with the lower house in making laws. All laws must have the approval of the Senate.

unique: being the only one of its kind; solitary.

urban: city.

vain: proud of one's abilities or looks.

valor: heroic courage.

vast: very great in area or extent; immense.

vibration: the condition of being vibrated, thus producing a sound.

violate: to break or disregard, as a law, rule or promise.

venture: an undertaking that is dangerous; daring or of doubtful outcome.

versus: in contrast with: i.e., coastal tribes versus the tribes of the desert.

vertebra: any of the bone or cartilaginous segments forming the spinal column.

vertical: at right angles to the horizon; upright.

volcanic: produced by or discharged from a volcano.

volcanic magma: the molten matter under the earth's crust from which igneous rock is formed by cooling.

vocational: related to being in training in a skill or trade to be pursued as a career.

warfare: violent or persistent conflict; as, warfare between neighbors.

wasteland: uncultivated or desolate country; a barren, ruined or ravaged land.

watertight: so assembled or constructed that water cannot enter or escape; waterproof.

wedge: a piece of a substance that tapers to a thin edge and is used for splitting wood and rocks, raising heavy bodies or for tightening by being driven in to something.

weir: a fence or enclosure placed in a stream to catch or retain fish.

wilds: an uncultivated, uninhabited or desolate region or tract.

winatun: a special helper for some Yokuts chiefs whose duty was to greet all travelers, discuss their business and, if necessary, take them to the chief.

winnow: to separate and drive off (as chaff) by subjection to wind or a current of air.

wretched: attended by misery and deep sorrow.

xonta: a plankhouse built by a family member in the Hupa tribe for shelter and a place to eat.

INDEX